28 Carols to Sing at Christmas

28 Carols to Sing at Christmas

John M. Mulder & F. Morgan Roberts

WITH A FOREWORD BY *Richard J. Mouw*

CASCADE *Books* · Eugene, Oregon

28 CAROLS TO SING AT CHRISTMAS

Cascade Books
An Imprint of Wipf and Stock Publishers
199 W. 8th Ave., Suite 3
Eugene, OR 97401

www.wipfandstock.com

ISBN 13: 978-1-4982-0682-2

Cataloging-in-Publication data:

Mulder, John M., and F. Morgan Roberts

    28 carols to sing at Christmas / John M. Mulder and F. Morgan Roberts.

    xviii + 182 p.; 23 cm.

    ISBN 13: 978-1-4982-0682-2

    1. Christmas music. 2. Carols. I. Title.

M2065 .M58 2015

Manufactured in the USA.

John M. Mulder dedicates this book to

Milton J. Coalter, Robert J. Donia, Walk C. Jones III,

James W. Lewis, Donald A. Luidens, W. Eugene March,

Randall M. Miller, Dianne Reistroffer, Grayson L. Tucker Jr.,

Louis B. Weeks, and Dirk Wierenga,

with deep gratitude for their invaluable gift of friendship.

F. Morgan Roberts dedicates this book

to his children, Hillie, David, Dwight, and Holly,

surprising gifts of God's amazing grace,

and delightful companions as we have walked together

through the winter wonderland

of many Christmases.

Contents

Acknowledgments

This book is a sequel to our work *28 Hymns to Sing Before You Die* (Cascade, 2014). Unfortunately, some people interpreted the title as hymns about death. What we meant to convey was that the book was a "bucket list" of favorite hymns. We enjoyed producing that resource for meditation so much that we decided to turn to Christmas carols. This time the title, *28 Carols to Sing at Christmas*, is less subject to misunderstanding.

We both are indebted to our wives for their encouragement and their editing—John's wife Mary and Morgan's wife Nora. We also appreciate the support of the staff at Cascade, especially our editor, Rodney Clapp, and James Stock and Matthew Wimer.

Half of the honoraria for this book will go to the Redlands Christian Migrant Association, 420 West Main Street, Immokalee, Florida. Through its two charter schools in Immokalee and Wimauma and its eighty-seven child care centers, it serves more than 8,000 farmworker children annually.

The resources for studying Christmas carols are rich and extensive. For those who want more background, here are some guides that might be helpful. *The New Oxford Book of Carols* (1992), edited by Hugh Keyte and Andrew Parrott, is the authoritative source, but it doesn't include some popular carols and can be overwhelming in its details. Ian Bradley's *The Penguin Book of Carols* (1999) is much more accessible and, on occasion, witty. Elizabeth Poston edited *The Penguin Book of Carols* (1965) and *The Second Penguin Book of Christmas Carols* (1970). They are brief volumes but helpful for carols not covered by Bradley.

William E. Studwell has devoted his life to studying carols, and the product of his labors can be found in *Christmas Carols: A Reference Guide* (1984), *The Christmas Carol Reader* (1995), and *An Easy Guide to Christmas Carols: Their Past, Present, and Future* (2006). Studwell also served as the editor of Ronald M. Clancy's lavishly illustrated books *Best-Loved Christmas Carols* (2000) and *American Christmas Classics* (2001).

The website www.hymnary.org is a herculean effort to bring together information about thousands of hymns, including carols, and it will be used gratefully by musicians, preachers, writers, and anyone interested in sacred song.

Denominations often issue what are called "companions" to a new hymnbook when it is published, and these are frequently valuable for short historical sketches about the carols in the hymnal and the individuals involved in their composition.

Finally, John M. Mulder is grateful to the libraries of Louisville Presbyterian Theological Seminary, Southern Baptist Theological Seminary, and Western Theological Seminary. Their collections of material about carols were invaluable.

Foreword

By Richard J. Mouw

In any given Advent season I can expect to hear at least one sermon featuring a complaint about "the commercialization of Christmas." I always agree with the basic concern being expressed. But I quietly dissented during one of those sermons when the preacher used as an example what he considered to be the distasteful practice of playing Christmas carols over the sound systems at shopping malls.

I love Christmas carols, and I even find it inspiring to hear them sung in shopping malls. Some lines in particular tempt me to stop in my tracks. When, surrounded by bustling crowds, I hear that "the hopes and fears of all the years are met in Thee tonight," I want to pause to try to imagine the ways in which the coming of Christ speaks to the deepest yearnings of the people in this particular mall. Or this line: "He comes to make his blessings flow far as the curse is found." Wow! Every experience, represented right there in Target, of the cursedness of our fallen world is something that the Babe of Bethlehem came to redeem.

The hymnbook has been a key resource in my spiritual journey. I have learned some of my best theology from the hymns we sang in my youth. Christmas carols, however, have a very special place in my consciousness. In the evangelical world where I spend most of my time, we sing more "contemporary Christian music" than we do the older standards. But not at Christmas time. The enduring presence of the carols in the worship of the younger generation is, I believe, a testimony to the worshipful quality of what we have received from the past regarding the birth of the Savior. I am all in favor of producing new music for the worshiping life of the church. But we might want to take our time a bit in writing new Christmas music until we are sure we have been serious about mining the riches we already have.

And that leads me to say that this book does some marvelous mining. I am going to keep it handy and reread portions regularly, especially during

Advent season—but not only then. John Mulder and Morgan Roberts are a
fine team for writing a book like this together. While they have divided the
labor between them, one providing commentary and the other devotional
reflection, they have not drawn the boundaries too strictly. Thank the Lord.
Roberts inspires as he informs, and Mulder informs as he inspires. The result is precious gift—and not just a Christmas gift, although I hope it finds
its place in some gift-giving early on in the Advent season! It is a treasure
to be cherished by all of us who continue to experience awe and wonder at
what happened at "the dawn of redeeming grace."

Introduction

It wouldn't be Christmas without Christmas carols.

Virtually every Christian would agree. The songs of Christmas can be heard from all kinds of media today, and they help make Christmas the biggest holiday in the United States and nearly every land where Christianity has a significant influence. The Christian church teaches that Easter is the most important event of the church year, but Christmas is what people truly celebrate. More than any aspect in this seasonal expression of joy and faith, music is what makes Christmas meaningful and memorable.

Our book has a simple purpose. We have designed a devotional aid—a book that can be read for insight and inspiration. We wrote it as a resource for increasing your faith in Jesus Christ and following the Savior of the world. So, you don't need to read this book "kiver to kiver," as the Scots would say. Instead, put it on your bedside table or next to your morning coffee and dip into it whenever you wish. We hope and pray that you will be changed as you read, just as Christ changed the world.

I

In some ways, the prevailing popularity of Christmas is a strange phenomenon. Our contemporary celebrations simply didn't happen or weren't very important throughout most of the history of the church. For example, consider the Bible. In the four Gospels, the birth of Jesus is covered well by Luke, somewhat by Matthew, and abstractly by John. Mark doesn't even mention it. Indeed, the overwhelming emphasis of the four Gospels focuses on the most important claim of the early Christians: Christ died and was resurrected from the dead. For nearly four centuries, Easter was the heart of the Christian story and the high point of the Christian year. Christmas did not count. Eventually, when Christmas became a significant holiday, church leaders often criticized the ways it was celebrated and condemned its excesses. The truth is that the Christian church has ironically vacillated in how much significance it attached to Christmas itself.

Scholars agree that "the birth of Christmas" came during the fourth century when a pagan festival for the sun god was taken over by Christians and declared sacred. In some ways, this is appropriate. It captures the idea of the incarnation—God becoming human, the secular being sanctified. But the origins of Christmas (literally "Christ" "mass") raise an age-old question that is still important today. Is this basically a secular holiday of feasting and giving gifts, or is it a religious day celebrating the gift of God's love in Jesus Christ?

The issue is complicated by the fact that we don't know when Jesus was born. In the second century, Clement of Alexandria publicly ridiculed any attempt to determine the date of Christ's birth. That didn't stop people from trying, and various dates were proposed—January 6, March 20, March 28, April 2, and December 25. January 6 was a strong contender because it traditionally marked the day of Christ's baptism, known as Epiphany. Gradually, December 25 was set as the date on the calendar, though to this day some members of the Eastern Orthodox Church observe Christmas on January 6.

Christmas also became popular with the people and had both sacred and secular dimensions. Within the church, the music of Christmas masses and liturgical dramas reenacted the birth of Jesus, but outside the church, grand feasts and drinking songs were signs of the season. During medieval times, the celebrations became steadily larger and more ostentatious. In the fourteenth century, Richard II of England threw a Christmas bash that lasted several days. More than 2,000 oxen and 200 barrels of wine were consumed by more than 10,000 people. The peasants loved Christmas because food was scarce during the winter. It's not clear who cleaned up after the parties were over.

From various parts of Europe emerged different Christmas traditions—mixtures of folk culture and Christmas practice. The French carol, which was originally a drinking song, came into the church and was transformed—especially later in England and the United States—into a form of religious music unique to Christmas. From Germany came the Christmas tree, and from England the holly and the ivy. The boar's head was originally a Scandinavian custom, adopted by the English. In many cultures, Christmas became associated with a festival of lights—similar to Hanukkah.

One prominent branch of Protestantism put the brakes on Christmas celebrations with dramatic consequences for British and American culture. Although Luther embraced Christmas, the Puritans despised it. From the sixteenth to the nineteenth century, the celebration of Christmas as a religious holiday in Britain and the United States declined, if not disappeared entirely. The Massachusetts Puritans even passed a law in 1659 declaring that "anybody who is found observing, by abstinence from labor, feasting or any other way, any such days as Christmas day, shall pay for every such offence five shillings." The law didn't last long. It was repealed in 1681, but Christmas didn't become a legal holiday in New England until 1856.

Three men helped change all this. In 1823 Clement C. Moore published "The Night Before Christmas." In 1834, Washington Irving introduced a laughing St. Nicholas and described an idealized Christmas in his *Sketch Book*. Most importantly, in 1843 Charles Dickens immortalized the theme of Christmas as charity and benevolence in *A Christmas Carol.* This new Christmas was adopted by merchants during the late nineteenth century, and today entire industries are dependent upon Christmas sales and related revenues.

One historian has flatly concluded, "The Christmas rituals that we enact are comparatively modern, just over one hundred years old." In addition, virtually every Christmas season sees an anguished reexamination of the season. Speakers and writers urge a return to the simplicity of an earlier Christmas or a recovery of the true meaning of Christmas—the coming of God in Jesus Christ to the world. The heart of Christmas is the mystery of God becoming human and its inspiring values of love and benevolence, especially for the poor. The celebration of Christmas is the ambiguity of a holiday of uncertain origin and conflicted meaning, wrapped in the warring impulses of greed and giving.

II

If it's difficult to understand Christmas, it's equally baffling to describe its music—what we call carols. The first significant carol, "Veni, Redemptor gentium" ("Savior of the Nations, Come"), is attributed to St. Ambrose in the late fourth century as Christmas began to develop. But for more than a thousand years, Christmas music was largely confined to the church and sung in Latin or Greek. Then people began to dance at Christmas, and St. Francis of Assisi and his followers encouraged a celebration that involved common people. Gradually, Christmas was becoming a festival of faith for all, and the democratization of the Yuletide season is perhaps the most important explanation for the rise of the carol in Christian worship and piety.

As you will see in this book, the breakthrough came during the eighteenth and nineteenth centuries in England and the United States. Inspired by the Bible, poets penned texts with scriptural themes but not in biblical verse. The explosion of music as entertainment prodded composers to write melodies that transformed the written word into poetry that could be sung and played. Long before Christ and Christmas, the author of Ecclesiastes observed, "Of the making of books there is no end" (12:12). The same is true of carols. They flowed like a mighty river, constantly gaining strength, into the twenty-first century.

There are various definitions of a carol, ranging from the very strict to the extremely broad. The editors of *The New Oxford Book of Carols* (1992) pronounce that a carol's "content must be narrative, contemplative, or celebratory, the spirit must be simple, the form normally strophic" (in other words, repetitive). The carol expert William E. Studwell maintains it is "a song used to celebrate Christmas and its adjacent events (including Advent, the New Year, Epiphany, and to some extent the winter season)." If your criteria are strict, then a number of "carols" drop out. If your criteria are broad, then a large number of songs are included ("Jingle Bells," "Have a Holly, Jolly Christmas," etc.) that would, we hope, never be sung in a church service.

Our criteria were very pragmatic. We focused on carols (or hymns or songs) with an explicitly Christian message. We pored through more than 100 hymnbooks, identifying the ones that have endured over time. We selected 28 carols to correspond with the four weeks of Advent. Most of the old "chestnuts, roasting on an open fire" are in this book. And then we threw criteria to the winds and included carols we loved, even if they don't often appear in many hymnbooks today (e.g., "Ah, Dearest Jesus" or "I Wonder as I Wander"), and gave a special place to the creativity of the unknown authors of African American spirituals. The arrangement is alphabetical by title, except for the conclusion: "O Holy Night."

III

Although each carol has its own characteristic emphasis, we found some themes that resonated throughout many, if not all, of the ones we selected. You will find your own meaning and significance in each carol, but we would like to highlight some themes as the enduring message of Christmas.

- *The cosmic love of God.* The God of Christmas is obviously a God of love, who became human to embrace the *cosmos* (Greek for "all creation"). Amidst the centuries of debate about the scope of God's salvation in Jesus Christ, the carols are virtually unanimous in affirming God's love for all. Amidst our contemporary concern about the environment, the carols proclaim that God's love extends even to all creation and all creatures, including animals.

- *The power of joy.* Perhaps no human emotion captures the spirit of Christmas more than the experience of rejoicing in God's love in Jesus Christ. The carols tell us this love is a gift. It is a divine extravagance for us who are seeking comfort and forgiveness, a magnificent display of God's benevolence for the entire world. For those who wrote the carols, it was more than happiness. It was pure, inexplicable, ineffable joy.

- *The awe of God.* In virtually every carol, if you listen closely, you will hear a poet and a musician straining to capture something mysterious and utterly beyond their own genius and creativity. Often it captures the paradox of Christmas—a Spirit becoming flesh, a God of majesty becoming poor, a compassion comforting the afflicted, a forgiveness extending to all. Listen and you will hear, but only partly understand.

- *The introspection of faith.* Heaven only knows what the facts of Christ's birth may have been. Carols also have a complex history that sometimes leaves us wondering who the author was, who wrote the music, and where they came from. But every carol ultimately says that though the facts may be contested, the truth is certain. And unless the fact of God's love in Jesus Christ becomes part of our inner selves, we know nothing of the truth that will set us free.

- *The gift of peace.* In a world as oppressive as that under Roman rule in the first century or in a world as violent as our own, Christmas represents a promise—a divine pledge that what is oppressively powerful will be brought low and what troubles the human soul will be vanquished. The beauty of "Silent Night" is both its vision of a different world in which all is calm and all is bright and its unquenchable hope that the peace of God will dwell within us.

- *The urgency of the news.* From the shepherds keeping watch over their flocks to the black slaves laboring in the fields, carols contain a message with a pressing proclamation:

"Be not afraid; for behold I bring you good news of a great joy
which will come to all the people; for to you is born this day
in the city of David a Savior, who is Christ the Lord" (Luke
2:10–11).

Christmas is a message to be received, but we cannot save what we do
not give away: "Go, Tell It on the Mountain."

Each reader will find insights into the Christian faith from these carols, but
all testify to the decisive way in which Christmas changed the world. As the
famous preacher Ralph Sockman declared, "The hinge of history is on the
stable door of Bethlehem."

Both of us have enjoyed writing this book, especially the wealth of
personal and family Christmas memories that working on it has evoked.
We hope that it will help inspire your own inner wonderland of Christmas
enchantment as it awakens the hopes and dreams of all the years in your
lives and families. Enjoy it and pass it on to your friends and, as you do,
wish them a Merry Christmas from us for many years to come. As Tiny
Tim declared in Dickens's *Christmas Carol*, "God bless us all, everyone."

John M. Mulder
F. Morgan Roberts

28 Carols to Sing at Christmas

Ah, Dearest Jesus, Holy Child

1. Ah, dear-est Je - sus, ho - ly Child, Make Thee a bed, soft, un - de - filed
2. My heart for ver - y joy doth leap, My lips no more can si - lence keep;
3. Glo - ry to God in high-est heaven, Who un - to man His Son hath given,

With - in my heart, that it may be A qui - et cham-ber kept for Thee.
I, too, must sing with joy - ful tongue, That sweet-est an - cient cra - dle song.
While an - gels sing with ten - der mirth, A glad new year to all the earth. A-MEN.

Ah, Dearest Jesus, Holy Child

This Christmas hymn was written by Martin Luther (1483–1546), undoubtedly one of the most important figures in the history of Christianity, Germany, and indeed the Western world. His influence extended far beyond the sphere of the church to politics, economics, education, and the arts.

Luther himself was a musician in voice and on instruments—the flute and the lute. In his advocacy of music in worship, he was a major factor in restoring congregational singing to worship and believed strongly in the spiritual power of music. "Next to the Word of God, the noble art of music is the greatest treasure in the world," Luther wrote. "It controls our thoughts, minds, hearts, and spirits."

Luther also declared, "I am strongly persuaded that after theology, there is no art that can be placed on a level with music; for besides theology, music is the only art capable of affording peace and joy of the heart, like that induced by the study of the science of divinity. A proof of this is that the devil, the originator of sorrowful anxieties and restless troubles, flees before the sound of music almost as much as before the Word of God."

The historian Philip Schaff has written, "To Luther belongs the extraordinary merit of having given to the German people in their own tongue the Bible, the Catechism, and the hymnbook, so that God might speak *directly* to them in His words, and that they might *directly* answer Him in their songs." The poet Samuel Taylor Coleridge flatly concluded that Luther "did as much for the Reformation by his hymns as he did by his translation of the Bible."

The tune, "Von Himmel Hoch," was probably written by Luther as well. He was fond of adapting folk tunes, including drinking songs, for religious purposes and is believed to have asked, "Why should the Devil have all the good music?" "Von Himmell Hoch" came from that German folk tradition. It was published in 1839 in a Leipzig hymnbook, *Geistliche Lieder*, and it has long been used with one of Luther's other carols, "From Highest Heaven I Come to Tell."

The translator of the hymn is the famous Catherine Winkworth (1827–1878), an Englishwoman who did more than anyone else to introduce German hymns into the worship lives of English-speaking people. In fact, she translated more than 400 German texts by about 170 authors.

Many hymnals have multiple hymns that were translated by her, including "Now Thank We All Our God," "Lift Up Your Heads, Ye Mighty Gates," "If Thou but Suffer God to Guide Thee," "Jesus, Priceless Treasure," "Praise Ye the Lord, the Almighty," and "Deck Yourself, My Soul, With Gladness."

Winkworth translated these German hymns for her own devotional use, not because she was hired by a publisher. She was part of the evangelical movement in nineteenth-century England, a social work pioneer, and an early and highly influential advocate of women's educational rights. She translated two German biographies of founders of sisterhoods for the poor and the sick, and her translations of hymns appeared in *Lyrica Germanica*. The first version (1855) went through twenty-three editions, the second version (1858) was published in twelve editions. She also wrote *The Chorale Book for England* (1863) and *Christian Singers of Germany* (1869).

Winkworth is a powerful figure in our hymnody and an example of the impact that women played in shaping our worship life, especially since the nineteenth century. As Erik Routley, a twentieth-century expert on hymnody, once observed, women have often known the contours of the human heart and the texture of faith better than men.

One historian has written of Winkworth, "She faithfully transplanted Germany's best hymns and made them bloom with fresh beauty in their new gardens." John Julian, the distinguished expert and editor of the landmark *A Dictionary of Hymnology*, declared, "Miss Winkworth, although not the earliest of modern translators of German into English, is certainly the foremost in rank and popularity. Her translations are the most widely used of any from that language, and have more to do with the modern revival of the use of German hymns than the versions of any other writer."

Despite persistent illness that kept her confined, she had a wide circle of friends, including the Brontë sisters. She died suddenly from heart disease. She said of her hymn translations that she hoped they "may speak to the hearts of some among us, to help and cheer those who must strive and suffer, and to make us feel afresh what a deep and true Communion of Saints exists among all the children of God in different churches and lands."

And so, from a robust reformer and a frail but courageous woman comes a haunting and beautiful carol that proclaims the Christmas exclamation of the ages:

> Glory to God in highest heaven,
> Who unto man His Son hath given,
> While angels sing with tender mirth,
> A glad new year to all the earth.

MEDITATION

You Did Not Grow Under My Heart But In It

My coauthor and I have many things in common, but one is very special: we are both adoptive parents. We have had the waiting experience of those whose children were brought to them from an adoption agency, and that is very different from that of parents whose waiting time is marked by the physical circumstances of pregnancy, which can entail various ups and downs and other anxieties.

The anxiety for us is that of awaiting telephone calls from the adoption agency, whether the first call that tells us that we have been "cleared" as eligible parents, or that final one that tells us that on a certain date a baby will be brought to our home.

The final day of arrival is an unforgettable experience. In the morning of that day our home is that of a childless couple; by nightfall, however, another little life has entered our life and our life will never be the same again. I still remember the arrival of my Hillie, who was brought to us on a snowy day, and how I first saw her eyes when the lady from the agency lifted the snowflake-covered blanket off her face. From that moment on, our home became wonderfully, beautifully quiet as we made a "bed, soft, undefiled" for her in our home and in our hearts. Everything in our life was suddenly different, changed forever by the presence of what seemed to us a "holy child."

As adopted children grow up and begin to ask how their arrival was different than that of their friends who came home in "the usual way," there is an adage that adoptive parents quote to them: "You did not grow under my heart, but in it." It is a lovely way to describe the specialness of their adoption.

As the years move on and those children grow up and move out into the world, that adage comes to have even deeper meaning for us as parents. My Hillie, as well as her adopted brothers and sister, have grown to have such a place in our hearts that it is almost inconceivable that it could have been any other way. We are certainly aware that, had we been at some other place at some other time, our children could have been adopted by some other couple. Given time, however, that possibility becomes unthinkable. It becomes impossible to believe anything other than that they were always in our hearts—that it was simply meant to be. I wonder if something like that becomes our experience of the presence of Jesus in our lives.

My wife Nora teaches the three-year-old Sunday school class at a Methodist church. While lessons vary from week to week, there is hardly a Sunday when she doesn't remind her pupils that Jesus is living in their hearts. "Where is Jesus?" she asks, and the children respond, "In our heart." Because we take this affirmation seriously, our children are baptized as infants to celebrate the fact that, by God's grace, before they even know who they are, these little ones are already the children of God.

When we think of our children in this way, we are really saying that we believe in the cosmic meaning of Christmas. We are saying that, when God entered our world in the person of Jesus, a divine Presence had secretly invaded every human life. Indeed, we are saying something even more than that; we are saying that God's presence in the life of Jesus was the living demonstration of what had always been true from the beginning—that every life bears the image of God, that all persons are children of God.

This certainly changes the meaning of Christmas; indeed, it changes life at all seasons. It means that we look upon everyone as a child of God, even if a particular person doesn't seem to live and act as though God's spiritual image is the central truth of their existence. "Even those who outwardly appear to deny Him are still His children, embraced in the arms of His love," wrote C. F. Andrews, the saintly Anglican missionary, whose life of devotion to the poor masses of India was praised by Gandhi. For that matter, Andrews recognized the presence of God in persons of other faiths, especially when their lives somehow demonstrated the love of Christ, even though they seemed to know God by another name.

Such a faith in the presence of the cosmic Christ in all of life explodes the meaning of Christmas by universal proportions. We henceforth "walk cheerfully over the world, answering that of God in every person," as the Quaker George Fox wrote. We know that, however outward appearances may seem to deny such a spiritual reality, the holy child Jesus is resting in some tiny, yet undiscovered, chamber at the back of every heart, awaiting discovery by God's grace in God's time. When that eureka moment arrives, such awakened souls will testify joyfully that, all along, the holy child Jesus was living in their heart. To believe that Jesus is living secretly in every heart makes Christmas a year-round experience!

Angels, From the Realms of Glory

1 An - gels, from the realms of glo - ry, wing your flight o'er all the earth;
2 Shep - herds, in the fields a - bid - ing, watch - ing o'er your flocks by night,
3 Sag - es, leave your con - tem - pla - tions, bright - er vi - sions beam a - far;
4 Saints be - fore the al - tar bend - ing, watch - ing long in hope and fear,

you who sang cre - a - tion's sto - ry, now pro - claim Mes - si - ah's birth:
God with us is now re - sid - ing, yon - der shines the in - fant light:
seek the great De - sire of na - tions, you have seen the na - tal star:
sud - den - ly the Lord, de - scend - ing, in his tem - ple shall ap - pear:

Come and wor - ship, come and wor - ship, wor - ship Christ, the new-born King.

Angels, From the Realms of Glory

Some of the greatest religious literature has come from individuals who served time in prison—e.g., the Apostle Paul, Dietrich Bonhoeffer, Martin Luther King Jr., and others. James Montgomery (1771–1854), the author of "Angels, From the Realms of Glory," falls into this group of incarcerated but venerated saints of the faith. Born to a family of Moravian missionaries, who died when he was a young boy, he suffered from depression during his entire adult life. Eventually he became the editor of *The Sheffield Iris*, a radical newspaper in Sheffield, England, for more than three decades. During that long tenure Montgomery was jailed twice, once for publishing a poem praising the fall of the Bastille in France and later for reporting on a political riot in Sheffield. In prison he wrote a book of poems, *Prison Amusements*.

Montgomery was both a political activist and an ardent evangelical. He lent his voice to reform movements, ranging from the abolition of slavery to the protection of chimney sweeps, and he vocally supported the work of the Bible Society and foreign missions. He called lotteries "a national nuisance," a warning ignored then and now.

After his paper was taken over by a political rival, he spent the last years of his life writing religious poetry. Many of his more than 400 poems became hymns, and more than one hundred are in contemporary use. He was, as one writer put it, "a poet by nature and a champion of human rights by vocation." He is regarded as third, following Isaac Watts and Charles Wesley, in his contribution to English hymnody. John Julian, the great musical scholar, concluded that Montgomery "bequeathed to the church wealth which could only come from true genius and a sanctified heart."

On Christmas Eve, 1816, "Angels, From the Realms of Glory" first appeared in Montgomery's newspaper as a poem, "Nativity." It is a loose paraphrase of a late-eighteenth-century folk hymn, "Les anges dans nos campagnes," that also inspired "Angels We Have Heard on High" (pp. 14–18) and "Shepherds in the Fields Abiding." The French hymn had a tune called "Iris," named after Montgomery's firebrand newspaper. Ironically,

"Iris" is a lovely, simple, graceful piece of music—a dramatic contrast to the pugilistic periodical Montgomery edited. It remains the preferred tune in Britain.

However, in the United States, "Angels, From the Realms of Glory" is sung to "Regent Square." Easier to sing than "Iris," "Regent Square" was composed by Henry Thomas Smart (1813–1879), and it was first published in 1867. Stewart went blind just two years before he wrote this stately, regal music, and after his affliction he dictated his music to his daughter. Smart was born in London and received his first musical training from his father, a violinist and music publisher. He flirted briefly with a career in law and turned down a commission in the army to pursue his passion—music. He became an accomplished organist and designer of organs and served several churches. One of those was the Regent Square Church in London, and he named this tune after that English Presbyterian congregation.

The composition of "Angels, From the Realms of Glory" winds its way from the bucolic fields of eighteenth-century southern France, to the political tumult of early-nineteenth-century England, to the worship life of late-nineteenth-century English churches. Today it is sung around the world. William E. Studwell, a distinguished scholar of Christmas carols, pronounced it "one of the finest pieces of the Christmas season" and said it "ranks in the highest echelon of sacred music." Another historian declared, "For comprehensiveness, appropriateness of expression, force and elevation of sentiment, it may challenge comparison with any hymn that was ever written, in any language or country."

Matthew believed genealogy mattered, so he began his Gospel by tracing "Jesus Christ, the son of David" back to Abraham. It is a tangled but awesome story of God's providence through many generations in diverse times and places. So it is with "Angels, From the Realms of Glory" and many other carols. From multiple sources and manifold experiences emerges something beautiful, powerful, and divine that reveals God's kind and merciful love in Christ—for us and for all—today.

MEDITATION

Just Doing Their Job

Here they come! Angels from the realms of glory come flying down to earth with the big news. These are the same angels who were singing at the creation of the world, but now they've been sent to announce an even greater event of re-creation—and where do they go? To the wrong place! Yes, to a group of fellows who have the worst possible job in the world of that day—some "shepherds in the fields abiding"! Sometimes I wonder if God couldn't have done it in a better way. God surely didn't know how to run a big enterprise, at least not in the way we would go about it.

Just take Jesus for example. Why "on earth" didn't God choose a better family in which to arrive in our world? Think how much more effectively, and how much more quickly, the same Jesus could have delivered God's message if he had been born, for example, into a priestly family. He would have been brought up with a more scholarly understanding of the Scriptures, and would have had impeccable connections. As a principal insider, he could have carried on his reforming work from the inside. But instead, Jesus was born to a poor family, and in a culturally uninspiring town. "Can anything good come out of Nazareth?" was the saying, which meant that Nazareth didn't offer great ways to enjoy the richness, wonder, and variety of life. There's even possible evidence to indicate that Nazareth may not even have had a synagogue in Jesus' day.

So God came into the world in the life of a man who spent most of his life up to the age of thirty doing the kind of manual work that, we hope, our sons or daughters will never have to perform. Most parents hope that their children will be able to "better themselves," but Jesus never did. Do you see what I mean when I say that God didn't go about managing the salvation enterprise by the kind of strategy that we would have pursued? When we want to get a big job done, we create an organization with a board of directors that are chosen because they are "key" people, people with business, managerial, or professional skills, and yes, of course, money. But during my half-century of service on the boards of colleges and seminaries, I've never been on a board in which a carpenter, plumber, or electrician ever served as a trustee or director.

So it is profoundly moving to me when I realize that God began the big job of saving the world by coming to the kind of people who were "just doing their job," and not a very impressive job at that. Of course, God had done the same thing before that night. God didn't come up with a plan for delivering the chosen people from slavery in Egypt while Moses had a princely position within Pharaoh's palace. God couldn't get the job done until Moses was a failed prince. And what was Moses doing when God broke the big news to him? Exactly the same as those shepherds in our Christmas story: tending sheep. Worse yet, Moses was working for his father-in-law, usually the "pits" of a job when your wife's father has to create work for you. Such as it was, Moses was just doing his job. What a way to begin saving a nation!

And then there's David. Saul was a failure as king; a new leader was needed for God's people, so Samuel was sent to the house of Jesse who lived in—guess where—Bethlehem, and Samuel didn't find the impressive leader for whom he was looking among the handsome sons of Jesse. "Is this all you've got?" (my paraphrase), he asked Jesse. Not quite; there was one more, the youngest son. Jesse didn't even bother introducing that little kid as a candidate. Besides, little David had a job to do on those hillsides outside of Bethlehem: "he is keeping the sheep," said Jesse. Sound familiar? He was doing the very same job in the very same place as those other shepherds on the night of Jesus' birth centuries later. Just doing his job!

God is not picky about the places where bushes burn, and kings are discovered, and "angels from the realms of glory" sing their song. God can come into your life anywhere. But I wonder if there's a clue here for all of us, especially for those of us who are "stuck," just doing what we have to do for a living, surviving in a situation we can't seem to escape, or facing a long road ahead that seems to be going nowhere. There was one liberating moment of experience that all shepherds could have out on those hills—and Jesus had it also at the end of every day in the carpenter's shop. We all have God's cathedral of creation.

Jesus must have resorted to that grand cathedral regularly. His parables are full of that natural imagery that could only have been learned by gazing upon the lilies of the field or by going up a mountain to pray. That same cathedral of creation is always awaiting you, and God will somehow speak to you there.

Next to me as I write are these words of Henry Van Dyke. I believe that they'll work for all of us. He entitled them, *The Foot-Path to Peace*, and this is what he wrote:

To be glad of life, because it gives you the chance to love and work and to play and to look up at the stars; to be contented with your possessions, but not satisfied with yourself until you have made the best of them; to despise nothing in the world except falsehood and meanness, and to fear nothing except cowardice; to be governed by your admirations rather than by your disgusts; to covet nothing that is your neighbour's except his kindness of heart and gentleness of manners; to think seldom of your enemies, often of your friends, and every day of Christ; and to spend as much time as you can, with body and spirit, in God's out-of-doors—these are little guide-posts on the footpath to peace.

Angels We Have Heard on High

1 An - gels we have heard on high sweet - ly sing - ing o'er the plains,
2 Shep - herds, why this ju - bi - lee? Why your joy - ous strains pro - long?
3 Come to Beth - le - hem, and see him whose birth the an - gels sing;

and the moun - tains in re - ply ech - o back their joy - ous strains.
Say, what may the ti - dings be which in - spire your heaven - ly song?
come, a - dore on bend - ed knee Christ the Lord, the new - born King.

Refrain

Glo - - - - - ri - a

in ex - cel - sis De - o! Glo - - - -

- - - ri - a in ex - cel - sis De - o!

14

Angels We Have Heard on High

Christmas is a mystery of manifold proportions, and this carol is shrouded in historical uncertainty. We know nothing about its author. One myth is that it was written in 129 CE at the order of Bishop Telesophorus, a story deemed "complete nonsense" by one expert. Scholars now agree that it arose in late-eighteenth-century rural France. Its original title was "Les anges dans nos campagnes" or "Angels in our mountains." This is a macaronic carol because it combines both English and Latin ("gloria in excelsis Deo"), and that probably means it was written by a priest or someone acquainted with both French and Latin.

It was known in both France and England by the early nineteenth century because James Montgomery used it in 1816 as the basis for "Angels, From the Realms of Glory" (pp. 8–13). It remained unpublished until 1855 when it appeared in *Nouveau Recueil de cantiques*. James Chadwick (1813–1882), a Roman Catholic bishop in England, published an imitation of the French original in 1860, and in 1862 an adaptation of that text was printed, with no attribution, in *Crown of Jesus Music*. In 1916 yet another translation appeared—again anonymously—and that is the version we use today.

The composer of the tune, "Gloria," is also unknown. What is evident is that it was arranged in its present form by Edward Shippen Barnes (1887–1958) for *The New Church Hymnal* (1937). Barnes was a distinguished American church musician with a career in the Presbyterian and Episcopal churches and wrote anthems, organ and choral pieces, and services for the Episcopal Church, and an organ method book.

William E. Studwell, an expert in Christmas carols, has written, "'Angels We Have Heard on High,' with conjecture and anonymity strewn throughout its historical path, is probably the most historically fragile of all the international-class Christmas carols," and yet it "is artistically at the top of the carol genre."

What are we to make of the historical mystery of "Angels We Have Heard on High"? For one thing, it is obvious that poets, composers, and publishers of the past were less preoccupied and more relaxed about the question of authorship than we are today. Creativity now warrants recognition and protection, and deservedly so.

But another explanation is possible. Every poet, composer, and performer eventually realizes that what they have done is larger than themselves. Its beauty is something that has come from beyond their imagination and transcends their creation. It is divine.

In the most-quoted story in the Bible, Jesus tells Nicodemus that he must be born again or born anew. Nicodemus is mystified and asks whether someone needs to enter a second time into a mother's womb and be born. Jesus replies, "Do not marvel that I said to you, 'You must be born anew [or again]. The wind blows where it wills, and you hear the sound of it, but you do not know whence it comes or whither it goes; so it is with every one who is born of the Spirit" (John 3:3–8).

As we sing a carol, as we ponder its meaning, let us give thanks for the artistic genius that created it. But let us also realize that its power lies in an inspiration from God and is enveloped in God's inexplicable desire that we be made whole. For the truth behind each carol is that "the wind blows where it wills, and you hear *the sound* of it, but you do not know whence it comes or whither it goes; so it is with *every one* who is born of the Spirit."

MEDITATION

Come to Bethlehem and See? No Thanks!

"You could have gone to the Holy Land and you went instead to Pittsburgh?" That was the amazed reaction of my friend, Norman Shapiro, when I told him that I'd declined the offer of a free trip to Israel because of a prior engagement in Pittsburgh. Norman was our neighborhood pharmacist and had told me about a tour of Israel from which he and his wife had just returned. As faithful Jews, they had visited Israel before, but this time they went with a Christian group to see it through Christian eyes. It was a great experience, and he was recommending it to me when I told him how I had turned down such a tour—and a free one at that.

A Holy Land tour brochure sits on our dining room table as I write these words; family members will be going on one. Yes, I'd like to go on one, especially with seminary faculty friends who could make it even more biblically/historically accurate than most tours. I can still decipher a tiny bit of Hebrew and could brush up on grammar and vocabulary to make it even more interesting. But still I won't be going; for that matter, I won't be going on any tour anywhere as much as I'd enjoy one, for example, to follow the footsteps of the Apostle Paul in Greece. My New Testament Greek proficiency is still fair, and I'd really enjoy that trip. But still, I'm not going; walking has become too demanding, and I'd be a drag on the younger tourists.

I'm not in a "sour grapes" mood when I make the following statement: I really wish I could tour the places where our Hebrew Christian traditions have their roots, but I've learned that I already live in the Holy Land—right here in my own holy (and sometimes unholy) neighborhood. It took me many years to realize this. When I first tried to witness to my newfound teenage faith to an older neighborhood lady, she seemed baffled by my complicated dogma. My faith was in doctrines about past happenings, of how Jesus took the rap for us so that, by accepting those creedal truths, we might gain entrance to a future heaven. But Beulah, a warm and wonderful friend who still attended her women's Sunday school class at the Reformed Church, told me that her faith was in a Jesus who was still with us today. I still remember her saying how she often felt that she could see Jesus walking in the fields whenever she drove through the countryside. Beulah (and I) did not realize how true her faith was to that of early Christians.

Early Christianity was not a "Holy Land tour" kind of faith; Peter and Paul didn't seem to feel any need to cling to Jerusalem, although some early Jewish Christians did. One school of faith wanted to keep Christianity Jewish. However, beginning with Peter's connection with the conversion of the Roman Centurion, Cornelius (Acts 10), and Paul's Damascus Road experience (Acts 9), Christianity became a faith that moved out into all the world. Jesus was out there in the faraway Gentile world, calling to them, as in Paul's vision, "Come over to Macedonia and help us" (Acts 16:9). And that same Jesus is still calling to us in our own neighborhoods.

I know that Jesus is alive and well in my small subdivision. He's working in some way in the home of that man who seems so domineering and aggressive. Jesus understands whatever it was in his childhood that made him feel that he always needs to be at war with the world. Besides, his wife is a gentle soul; she must have seen something gentle in his heart. Then there's that other woman who seems like a witch—no one seems to like her, but I don't think Jesus will ever give up on her. The big surprise was when I got to know the man who was called "evil" by another neighbor. He wasn't evil, just a bit certain in expressing his opinions. Probably some experience from his childhood has created a hunger for recognition so that his convictions are sometimes overstated. He is trying to live by the dictates of his faith and conscience. I do not doubt that Jesus lives somewhere in his heart and home.

Jesus is wherever we are. When we read that "the Word became flesh and lived among us" (John 1:14 in which the Greek is very pictorial, "pitched his tent among us"), it means that Jesus came to stay. He's still here and recognizable through eyes of faith to those who are looking for Him.

George MacDonald's *Sir Gibbie* is a lovely tale about an orphan shepherd boy who is "loved into" a personal faith in Jesus by a Scottish peasant lady. Gibbie's world now seems filled with Jesus. Gibbie "would dream waking dreams about Jesus, gloriously childlike. He fancied he came down every now and then to see how things were going in the lower part of his kingdom. . . . Then high and fast would his heart beat at the thought that some day he might come upon his path just when he had passed, see the heather lifting its head from the trail of his garment. Sometimes, when a sheep stopped feeding and looked up, he would fancy that Jesus had laid his hand on its head, and was now telling it that it must not mind being killed; for he had been killed, and it was all right."

"Come to Bethlehem and see." No, I won't be going, but I wish my friends well on their Holy Land tour. I have all the holy land I need right here where I live—and so do you!

Away in a Manger

Cradle Song

1 A - way in a man-ger, no crib for a bed, the lit - tle Lord
2 The cat - tle are low-ing, the Ba - by a - wakes, but lit - tle Lord
3 Be near me, Lord Je - sus; I ask thee to stay close by me for -

Je - sus laid down his sweet head; the stars in the bright sky looked
Je - sus, no cry - ing he makes. I love thee, Lord Je - sus, look
ev - er, and love me, I pray. Bless all the dear chil-dren in

down where he lay, the lit - tle Lord Je - sus a - sleep on the hay.
down from the sky and stay by my side un - til morn-ing is nigh.
thy ten - der care, and fit us for heav-en, to live with thee there.

Away in a Manger

1 A - way in a man-ger, no crib for a bed, the lit - tle Lord
2 The cat - tle are low-ing, the Ba - by a - wakes, but lit - tle Lord
3 Be near me, Lord Je - sus; I ask thee to stay close by me for -

Je - sus laid down his sweet head; the stars in the sky looked
Je - sus, no cry - ing he makes. I love thee, Lord Je - sus, look
ev - er, and love me, I pray. Bless all the dear chil-dren in

down where he lay, the lit - tle Lord Je - sus a - sleep on the hay.
down from the sky and stay by my side un - til morn-ing is nigh.
thy ten - der care, and fit us for heav-en, to live with thee there.

Away in a Manger

This carol is a perennial favorite of the Yuletide season. In 1996 a Gallup poll in Britain on the ten most popular Christmas carols had it ranked in second place, tied with "O Come, All Ye Faithful."

I confess that, like many people, I made the mistake of associating "Away in a Manger" with Martin Luther. Luther loved music and wrote thirty-seven hymns. Music was an integral part of Luther's home and the Lutheran churches of his day and ever since.

So, it makes a certain amount of sense to attribute "Away in a Manger" to Luther. He actually did write five carols, including "Ah, Dearest Jesus, Holy Child" (pp. 2–7), so he certainly could have or perhaps should have composed this beloved Christmas classic. Alas, he didn't. Scholars now agree that we simply don't know who wrote it.

It first appeared, believe it or not, in a Universalist Church publication in 1884. Describing it as "Luther's Cradle Song," the article maintained that "Martin Luther, the great German reformer who was born four hundred years ago the 10th of next November, composed the following hymn for his children; and it is still sung by many German mothers to their little ones." The 400th anniversary of Luther's birth was actually 1883, not 1884, so the article was wrong about both Luther's authorship and his birthday.

It is possible that it came from Pennsylvania Lutherans. The first two verses were published in an Evangelical Lutheran Sunday school book, *Little Children's Book for Schools and Families* (1884). The third verse appeared in *Gabriel's Vineyard Songs* in 1892, published with tunes by Charles H. Gabriel, who was probably the author. The three verses together, with inevitable editorial changes, constitute "Away in a Manger" as we sing it today.

Forty-one different tunes have been used with "Away in a Manger," but two hold sway. One, known as "Mueller" or "Away in a Manger," was written by James R. Murray and published in 1887. Murray was a former student of Lowell Mason (pp. 80–81) and labored as a composer and music publisher. Murray's tune is most popular in the United States. In 1895 William J. Kirkpatrick composed the second tune, "Cradle Song," and it has its greatest usage in Great Britain and Canada. Today many hymnals use both tunes—one a quiet, reverential melody and the other an irenic, joyful song.

Commenting on "Away in a Manger," one author has suggested: "For sheer beauty and childlike simplicity the carol claims special attention. It is a gentle lullaby, tender and warm, especially loved by children; and when adults of any age sing it, they become children again."

Christmas celebrates the birth of the infant Jesus, who later called a child to his side and said to his disciples: "Truly I tell you, unless you change and become like children, you will never enter the kingdom of heaven. Whoever becomes humble like this child is the greatest in the kingdom of heaven. Whoever welcomes one such child in my name welcomes me (Matthew 18:3–4).

At Christmas, we become children of God and recognize the birth of Jesus with childlike awe. We are brought to our knees in humility and summoned to stand and care for all God's children.

MEDITATION

The Cattle Are Lowing

In Luke's account of the birth of Jesus, there is no mention of any cattle "lowing." Farm animals could have been there; why else would there have been a cattle trough for Jesus' bed? But the Greek word can also mean "stall" or just a feeding place under the sky. Still, the animals belong there, and the author of this carol must have known more about animals in the Bible than we realize. At the great moments of salvation in our Scriptures animals are, interestingly, always present.

In the story of Noah and the great flood, more animals are saved than people! And in Isaiah's vision of the peaceable kingdom, all kinds of creatures are present, objects of God's love and care. The most striking example, however, is in the story of Jonah, at the conclusion of which God saves not only the unenlightened people of Nineveh "who do not know their right hand from their left," but also "much cattle." God's mercy for the animals is added as a pointed punch line, as though to say to God's pouting prophet, "Did you really expect me to kill all those innocent beasts just to pander to your patriotic piety?"

We think of God's salvation as focused principally upon people, whereas the God of the Bible appears to be as concerned with the salvation of animals as with that of people. When we pray, "Thy kingdom come," do we envision a redeemed animal kingdom? Unless we have a broader vision for evangelism, a dream of good news for the earth that is as concerned with saving animals as it is with saving souls, we cannot claim to be God's kingdom people. Reverence for life must be reverence for all of life. Our spiritual wholeness is dependent upon our having a whole relationship with all of God's creatures.

I see this demonstrated whenever I see a homeless man begging on a busy city street corner with a faithful dog at his side. Despite deep debt, he holds on to some small coin of human dignity by having one living treasure that is all his, one faithful fellow creature that will not forsake him. His are the riches of spiritual wealth beyond that of the CEO who sits twenty stories above in his office tower who couldn't possibly be bothered with the care of any animal. In his barren "busyness" with the bottom line, he is isolated from the many splendored creatures pictured in Isaiah's vision. Busier than the God of creation who somehow finds time to mark the sparrow's fall, he couldn't possibly pause to "look at the birds of the air" as Jesus evidently learned to do, and urged his followers to do likewise.

If our concerns are so big that we have never been captivated by the brilliance of a butterfly, never enjoyed a moment of merriment in the acrobatics of a squirrel, or had our hearts warmed by a child's delight in a new puppy or kitten, can we enter the heavenly kingdom whose true citizens are the least and the little?

Chained to his desk at the counting house, the CEO may be dangerously close to the callous concept that, if there are creatures of lesser worth, then perhaps there are also people of lesser worth whose lands can be bombed and burned with impunity, Ninevites "who do not know their right hand from their left," who are just pawns in the great games of nations.

Thank goodness for that one holy season of the year when we enter that stable in which the cattle are lowing, that gentler world in which a baby born in poverty is safe, that larger kingdom in which the ox and the ass become our brothers and sisters, all family members of our Father's peaceable kingdom.

Come, Thou Long Expected Jesus

Hyfrydol

1 Come, thou long - ex - pect-ed Je - sus, born to set thy peo-ple free;
2 Born thy peo - ple to de - liv - er, born a child and yet a king,

from our fears and sins re - lease us; let us find our rest in thee.
born to reign in us for - ev - er, now thy gra - cious king-dom bring.

Is-rael's strength and con-so - la - tion, hope of all the earth thou art;
By thine own e - ter - nal Spir-it rule in all our hearts a - lone;

dear De - sire of ev - ery na - tion, Joy of ev - ery long-ing heart.
by thine all - suf - fi - cient mer - it raise us to thy glo-rious throne.

24

1 Come, thou long - ex - pect - ed Je - sus, born to set thy peo - ple free;
2 Is - rael's strength and con - so - la - tion, hope of all the earth thou art;
3 Born thy peo - ple to de - liv - er, born a child and yet a king,
4 By thine own e - ter - nal Spir - it rule in all our hearts a - lone;

from our fears and sins re - lease us; let us find our rest in thee.
dear de - sire of ev - ery na - tion, joy of ev - ery long - ing heart.
born to reign in us for - ev - er, now thy gra - cious king - dom bring.
by thine all - suf - fi - cient mer - it raise us to thy glo - rious throne.

Come, Thou Long Expected Jesus

This inspiring hymn was written by Charles Wesley, the greatest hymn-writer in the English language. Technically, it isn't about Christmas itself but Advent—the season in which we anticipate and especially long for the birth of the Savior of the world. It belongs in a book of Christmas carols because it is the most profound of all the Advent hymns and captures so beautifully and deeply the quest of the human heart for God's presence.

Wesley (1707–1788) was a fountain of sacred poetry. During his lifetime, he poured forth more than 6,500 hymns (an average of eighty for every year he lived or more than one a week) and published sixty-four different hymnbooks. His brother, John Wesley, is better known to history as the primary founder and leader of Methodism, which has transformed Protestantism and indeed all of global Christianity.

However, Charles played an important part as well, and the fact is that virtually no one reads John Wesley's sermons today but millions around the world sing Charles Wesley's hymns. Some of his hymns are the greatest in the history of the church, and he is rightly called "the sweet Bard of Methodism."

Henry Ward Beecher, the so-called "prince of the Victorian pulpit," once said, "I would rather have written that hymn of Wesley's, 'Jesus, Lover of My Soul,' than to have the fame of all the kings that ever sat on the earth." The great hymnologist, John Julian, concluded that "perhaps, taking quantity and quality into consideration [Charles Wesley was] the greatest hymnwriter of all ages."

To comprehend the Wesleys, you need to understand their mother, Susanna Wesley, one of the most remarkable women in church history. Susanna Wesley was a woman of prodigious piety and extraordinary order. Their father, Samuel, was a somewhat prickly rector in the Church of England, but their mother was a woman of beauty, learning, efficiency, and piety.

She gave birth to nineteen children, only ten of whom survived beyond infancy. She educated all her children—not simply in the three R's but also in Latin, Greek, history, literature, and of course religion. She set aside one evening a week for each of the children to discuss their educational and spiritual development.

When John and Charles left for Oxford, they continued this disciplined approach to the Christian life. Their small group meetings of students focused on concentrated study and training each other in the spiritual life, and so they were derisively called "Methodists" because of their "methods."

Like Isaac Watts (pp. 77–81), Charles was attacked during his lifetime for abandoning Psalm singing in favor of hymn singing, and like Watts, he drew his hymns from the his vast knowledge of Scripture. For example, the basis for "Come, Thou Long Expected Jesus" was Haggai 2:7: "And I will shake all nations, so that the treasures ["desire"—King James Version] of all nations shall come in, and I will fill this house with splendor, says the Lord of hosts." That's hardly a text most people would know or associate with Advent.

Wesley was also criticized for his theology, which placed an emphasis on the human will in assenting to God's love and offer of salvation. This position, known as Arminianism, was an issue for all the Methodists and still strikes a tension between Methodism and some other traditions.

Watts was more of a Calvinist and wrote hymns that were objective and yet true. Wesley was more of an Arminian and wrote hymns that were subjective and yet true. One spoke more to the head, the other spoke more to the heart.

Both John and Charles Wesley remained ordained priests in the Church of England throughout their lives—despite deep strains between them and most of the rest of the Church of England. John was the itinerant minister and organizational genius of Methodism. His ministry lasted for fifty years—into his eighties—and he traveled more than 250,000 miles and preached 40,000 to 50,000 sermons. He gave Methodism its order.

Like John, Charles also itinerated as a preacher, but he gave Methodism its ardor. Because of Charles's focus on the poetic depiction of faith, the early Methodists were sarcastically described as those "singing Methodists."

Charles was almost obsessive about composing his hymns for the Methodists, often scribbling them on horseback. One day when his horse fell on him and he sprained his wrist, he complained that the horse had "spoiled my hymn writing for that day." He suffered from illness during his entire life, but he kept preaching and writing. On his death bed, he dictated a hymn of praise for his wife.

He also sought with persistence the right tunes to go with his poetry. The effort paid off. One contemporary wrote about the early Methodist gatherings: "Never did I hear such praying or such singing. Their singing was not only the most harmonious and delightful I ever heard, but they sang 'lustily and with a good courage.' . . . If there be such a thing as heavenly music upon earth I heard it there."

Another contemporary said, "The song of the Methodists is the most beautiful I ever heard. . . . They sing in a proper way, with devotion, serene mind, and charm."

In 1853 the *London Quarterly* concluded that Charles Wesley "was, perhaps, the most gifted minstrel of the modern Church."

In contemporary hymnals, Charles Wesley's genius is always bountifully represented by such hymns as "Hark, the Herald Angels Sing" (pp. 52–57), "Jesus Christ is Risen Today," "Rejoice, the Lord Is King," "Christ the Lord Is Risen Today," "Love Divine All Love's Excelling," "Come, Thou Almighty King," "Jesus, Lover of My Soul," and many others.

Perhaps his most famous hymn is "O for a Thousand Tongues to Sing," which is the national anthem of Methodism and always appears as hymn number one in Methodist hymnals. It was written on the first anniversary of his conversion as a joyful recollection of his new life in Christ.

"Come, Thou Long Expected Jesus" has been set to many tunes, but the two most popular are "Hyfrydol" and "Stuttgart." "Hyfrydol" was written by Rowland Hugh (or Huw) Pritchard (1811–1887), a musician from Wales, which despite its size has given the church many of its greatest hymns and most eloquent preachers. Written before Pritchard was twenty years old, "Hyfrydol" means "cheerful." He intended it for the handbook that accompanied his children's hymnal, *Cyfaill y Cantorium* ("The Singer's Friend"). It is often sung with another Wesley hymn, "Love Divine, All Love's Excelling," and it is by far my favorite hymn tune because, with the exception of only one note, it ranges across only five notes of the scale (thus accommodating my limited range).

The other common tune is "Stuttgart," written by Christian Friedrich Witt (1660–1716), a prolific German church musician. He was educated in music at any early age by his father and received advanced training in counterpoint and composition in Nuremberg. He went on to write both vocal and instrumental music, including sixty-five church cantatas. His most significant achievement was publishing (with A. C. Ludwig) a highly influential hymnbook, *Psalmodia sacra* (1716), consisting of 774 chorales with 356 melodies and more than one hundred new tunes, most of them by Witt. "Stuttgart" was one of those tunes.

In the midst of all this historical background, it's important to recognize that when Charles Wesley wrote "Come, Thou Long Expected Jesus," he wasn't celebrating an event long ago but imploring Christ to awaken our hearts anew. The hymn isn't about history. It's about now—today.

MEDITATION

No Waiting!

I couldn't agree more with my coauthor's final comment: "It's about now—today." That truth can somehow be overlooked because many of us observe a liturgical calendar in which, when we're approaching Christmas, we observe four Sundays as a time called Advent, during which we sing hymns in which we seem to be waiting for the coming of Jesus. Of course, it's not quite that way at all. We're just remembering those days of old when Israel was awaiting its "strength and consolation," the Messiah. Even though Jesus has come, we reenact those ancient years of waiting.

Many Christians, however, still seem to think that the big events are yet to come. They talk as though escaping hell and getting into a future heaven is the main agenda of Christian faith. It is, for them, what Christianity is about. For them, Christianity is basically an evacuation plan for escaping the fires of hell. We must admit that some people might never have become Christians had it not been for fear of hell. Their lives were so messed up that they needed to be frightened into faith. Hopefully, they will grow beyond such fear-based faith; however, some never do. Still, they are God's children—God's fearful children.

Many other Christians of simple faith do not live in such fear. As children, they were taught that Jesus loved them and they should love one another. They still look forward to a future heaven, but are content to believe that loving one another in the name of Jesus is the best way to live on every day, leaving the future with God.

Getting into heaven was not the main agenda of Jesus. In the prayer that he taught his disciples (and us), we pray for the coming of God's kingdom (rule) and the doing of God's will on earth now. Bringing the kingdom of heaven to earth was Jesus' principal concern. And Jesus declared repeatedly that it had already begun, that God's kingdom had already arrived, and was indeed "at hand."

Across all denominational differences, the great divide of faith is between those who are still waiting for the big events to happen, and those who believe that the living Christ is already here, that the realization of God's rule is happening in our world today. For people who believe that the triumphant Christ is present in all of life, heaven is not a place out there in the future, but instead, a present reality. As Dorothy Day wrote, "Heaven is not a place [but] a condition of soul—the vision of God, union with God. . . . It can begin here."

We arrive in heaven when, all of a sudden, we realize that we've been in it all along! We discover, as did St. Catherine of Siena, that "All the Way to heaven is Heaven, because He said I am the Way." Heaven begins when we discover that, right now, we live in an enchanted world, a world "wonder-filled" by our realization that the risen, ever-present Christ, is here today, secretly present and seeking to be recognized in every life. Because we live in the eternal now of God's presence, we know that we live in a safe and happy neighborhood, a world in which God is "at home," and that nothing can separate us from this powerful and loving God. Let me try to describe this safe and happy neighborhood in different terms.

It took me many years to realize that my parents were wealthy and that I had been brought up as a child of privilege. Of course, they weren't wealthy in the usual sense. It was quite the opposite. Several years ago, I discovered that I could access the 1940 census online. What I learned was that in the previous year of 1939, my father's annual salary was a huge $1,300. During my junior high school years we were living on little more than $100 per month. No wonder that our 1927 car remained in the garage unrepaired; my father couldn't afford to fix it. So that's why we always traveled by public bus and regularly ate chicken rather than steak.

What is amazing is that I never realized any of this. I can't remember wanting anything I didn't already possess. I had my bicycle, my ice skates, and my chickens in the backyard coop. I had friends and kindly teachers at school. What more could any kid desire in life? And most of all, I had loving parents who gave me lots of trust and freedom—and who never argued over money. I was in heaven all along, and it took me years to realize it.

"This is my Father's world," wrote preacher/poet Maltbie Babcock. We're already in the kingdom of God, already in all the heaven that we need. There'll be more in the future, but we have all the heaven we need for today. We're not waiting for some big event in the future. Jesus has already come, and he came to stay. This world is God's world—now. So we can start putting a new sign outside our churches: NO WAITING!

Gentle Mary Laid Her Child

1. Gen - tle Mar - y laid her Child Low - ly in a man - ger;
2. An - gels sang a - bout His birth, Wise Men sought and found Him;
3. Gen - tle Mar - y laid her Child Low - ly in a man - ger;

There He lay, the Un - de - filed, To the world a stran - ger.
Heav - en's star shone bright - ly forth Glo - ry all a - round Him.
He is still the Un - de - filed, But no more a stran - ger.

Such a Babe in such a place, Can He be the Sav - iour?
Shep - herds saw the won - drous sight, Heard the an - gels sing - ing;
Son of God of hum - ble birth, Beau - ti - ful the sto - ry;

Ask the saved of all the race Who have found His fa - vor.
All the plains were lit that night, All the hills were ring - ing.
Praise His name in all the earth, Hail! the King of Glo - ry! A - MEN.

Gentle Mary Laid Her Child

This Christmas hymn won a contest. It was written by Joseph Simpson Cook (1859–1933), a Canadian pastor who contributed articles and poems to many church-related publications.

In 1919, the Methodist magazine *Christian Guardian* sponsored a competition for Christmas carols and hymns. Cook wrote a poem, "The Manger Prince," and addressed the role of Mary, hardly a staple of Protestant Christmas celebrations. Perhaps because of its novelty, it was awarded first prize. Cook stopped there and never wrote another hymn.

Cook was born in Durham County, England, and migrated to Canada when he was a young boy. He became a Methodist and was educated at Wesleyan Theological College and Illinois Wesleyan University. His ministry was typical of Methodist preachers of that era—twelve short pastorates in Ontario over forty-four years. He became a minister of the United Church of Canada when the Canadian Methodists joined with other denominations in 1925.

The tune, "Tempus Adest Floridum," is a late medieval composition, which was first published in Sweden in 1582 as part of a collection of medieval songs and carols. The tune was attached to a spring carol, "Spring Has Now Unwrapped the Flowers," and the title means "the flowering time is near." It is the same tune used for "Good King Wenceslas," a very popular Christmas carol that rarely appears in contemporary hymnals because it is primarily a morality tale about charity, not a song about the birth of Christ.

The arrangement was written by Ernest (Alexander) Campbell MacMillan (1893–1973), one of the most distinguished musicians of the twentieth century. He was born in Canada and educated in Canada, Scotland, England, and France. During World War I he was a prisoner of war for four years. In the prison camp he composed music and in 1918 received a Doctor of Music from Oxford University *in absentia*. He also studied history while a prisoner and received an MA from the University of Toronto even before his release. He held many distinguished music posts in both church and academic circles and received honorary doctorates from nine universities in the United States and Canada. In 1935 he was knighted—the first person outside the British Isles to be honored in this way.

The words and tune of "Gentle Mary Laid Her Child" are easily sung and understood by children—a happy match of words and notes. If you stumble over "the race" in the first verse, please know that it refers to "the human race."

Because it appeals to singers young and old, "Gentle Mary Laid Her Child" captures the eloquent story of an impoverished woman giving birth to the child who brought the richness of love to all the world. To any who ask whether

> Such a Babe in such a place,
> Can He be the Savior?

It fervently proclaims:

> Ask the saved of all the race
> Who have found His favor.

MEDITATION

Gentle?

Whoever came up with the idea of describing Mary as "gentle"? We've probably never thought much about it, but she doesn't fit the usual definitions. The very first definition of "gentle" in my dictionary is "belonging to the upper classes of polite society," suggesting that gentle people are refined, educated, and schooled in good taste and manners. It's the picture of those who are genteel and know which fork to use at a formal dinner.

Neither Mary nor Joseph could fit that definition. When we read that Jesus and his father were carpenters (Mark 6:3), we must not envision the well-paid, high-end, union carpenters or cabinetmakers of our own time. To be a *tekton* was to be a member of that class who had lost their land and were reduced to working for other people. Indeed, such construction workers were of a lower class than the peasants who still had the minimal dignity of owning a small piece of land. And with an estimated 95 percent of the Jewish population being illiterate in those times, the probability of either Mary or Joseph being able to read is highly unlikely.

It is remarkable that God's landing on earth was not among "our kind" of people. Neither Mary nor Joseph look like the kind of people we usually see in church on Sunday morning. The ushers would not have escorted them to the front pews in the sanctuary; they would not be encouraged to attend the adult Sunday school class, nor to remain for the coffee hour after worship. When God decided to become one of us and walk upon our earth, it was not among gentlefolk who were prosperous and well-educated—and the holy family would certainly not "fit in" on a seminary campus.

So why employ the word "gentle" to describe Mary? The other definition of "gentle" is "not violent," but does that fit when we reflect upon the words of her famous song, the *Magnificat* (Luke 2:46–55)? It does not strain my imagination that a poor, illiterate Hebrew girl could sing such a song. Even in illiterate cultures, there can be a wealth of folk songs, and Mary's song echoes Hannah's song over the birth of Samuel (1 Sam 2:1–10.) People who cannot read can still sit around campfires, singing the old songs of their people, and if their people are poor and oppressed, the songs may be songs of protest. In such songs, God "has scattered the proud, brought down the powerful from their thrones, and lifted up the lowly; filled the hungry with good things, and sent the rich away empty" (Luke 1:51). Such songs of gentle, nonviolent protest have always been threatening to the powerful. Even in our own times, this song of Mary was considered so subversive by the Argentine government that it was banned from public recitation at protest marches.

What is it about such gentle, nonviolent folk that strikes fear in the hearts of the powerful? Such gentle force has tremendous power. Mary (and all of her sisters and brothers throughout history) was never passive. As Sister Joan Chittister writes, "Pacifism is not passivism." Mary is persistent in resisting evil powers. People like Mary act with clean, clear purpose. They focus upon issues without demeaning those with whom they disagree. They absorb physical attacks without striking back physically. They confound their enemies by actually loving them and seeking to make friendships with them. If you kill such people, they go down loving you, following the example of the one who prayed that those crucifying him be granted forgiveness (Luke 23:34). Evil empires simply cannot conquer Mary and her gentle friends because their persistence is based upon the inevitable victory of another empire, the kingdom of God, whose coming cannot be hindered.

Gentle Mary calls us to another kind of gentleness—a calm, determined, and unwavering devotion to the coming of God's just, righteous, and peaceable kingdom. That is, after all, what we pray for every Sunday when we repeat, "Thy Kingdom come, Thy will be done on earth." But that, of course, demands that we renounce allegiance to those other worldly empires that are based upon power, prestige, and possessions, the very idols that can rule our personal lives. It demands that we believe in Mary's kind of gentleness, that rare kind of gentleness described by the Psalmist, "Thy gentleness hath made me great" (Ps 18:35).

Go, Tell It on the Mountain

Go, tell it on the moun-tain, o-ver the hills and ev-ery-where;
go, tell it on the moun-tain that Je-sus Christ is born.

Parts

1 While shep-herds kept their watch-ing o'er si-lent flocks by night,
2 The shep-herds feared and trem-bled when, lo! a-bove the earth
3 Down in a low-ly man-ger the hum-ble Christ was born,

to Refrain

be-hold, through-out the heav-ens there shone a ho-ly light.
rang out the an-gel cho-rus that hailed our Sav-ior's birth.
and God sent us sal-va-tion that bless-ed Christ-mas morn.

Go, Tell It on the Mountain

This is one of the African American spirituals, earlier known as Negro spirituals or black spirituals. Calling them "African American spirituals" isn't simply an accommodation to common usage. It is historically more accurate.

Since the 1950s, there has been an explosion of scholarship on the history of the Africans who were enslaved by Western powers and the slavery they endured. That scholarship destroyed the "magnolia myth" of slavery as a benign institution. It also revealed the complexity of slavery and the manifold ways in which slaves found ways to survive amidst oppression.

One of their resources for endurance was religion. Historians vigorously debate when and how slaves became Christian, but some things are clear. White slaveholders and ministers were deeply ambivalent about evangelizing the slaves. They wanted slaves to learn Christianity's teaching about obedience and submission, not its proclamation of freedom and justice. But what whites desired and what slaves developed were two different expressions of faith. Slaves blended their African traditions and slave experience into something that was African American Christianity, not Euro-American Christianity. The overwhelming theme was a God who brought liberation to his people—both in this world and the next. Nowhere is that theme more powerfully expressed than in the songs they sang, such as:

> Go down Moses, way down in Egypt's land,
> Tell old Pharaoh, Let my people go!

We do not know the origins of these African American spirituals or songs of the Spirit. Scholars debate whether they drew on white folk songs or African chants, but it seems fairly clear that most of the spirituals arose out of African musical traditions and the slaves' profound understanding of the Bible. Eventually, the music and tunes of the songs were written down. By the mid-twentieth century they began to move beyond the walls of the black church and into the music life of Christians around the world.

The history of "Go, Tell It on the Mountain" illustrates the painful yet inspiring story of the African American spiritual. After the Civil War, the American Missionary Association founded Fisk University in Nashville, Tennessee, to educate freed slaves. The school created the Fisk Jubilee Singers, who traveled the country and were often banned from hotels, restaurants, train stations, and churches. When they sang the spiritual songs of slavery, they relied not on published music but the oral traditions of their enslaved ancestors. The Fisk Jubilee Singers won acclaim. They sang before Queen Victoria, William Gladstone, and Edward, Prince of Wales, in 1873 and often appeared on the platform of the revivalist Dwight L. Moody. Tragically, they felt they sometimes had to adapt their songs to the sensibilities of white audiences.

In the early twentieth century, John Wesley Work II (1872–1925) conducted the choir. He taught Latin and Greek at Fisk, and with his brother, Frederick Jerome Work (1879–1942), pursued their true calling of assembling and publishing the words and music of the slave spirituals, including *New Jubilee Songs as Sung by Fisk Jubilee Singers* (1901) and *Folk Songs of the American Negro* (1907). John Wesley Work II's pioneering analysis of slave music, *The Folk Song of the American Negro,* was published in 1915.

His son, John Wesley Work III (1902–1967), is probably the one who arranged the text and music for "Go, Tell It on the Mountain." Like his father and uncle, he devoted himself to teaching music and scholarship at Fisk. In 1940 he published the authoritative *American Negro Songs and Spirituals* (1940), a work scholars still consult regularly. As with other African American spirituals, "Go Tell It on the Mountain" was surely not composed but codified by Work from oral traditions that extend deeply into the slave experience of the nineteenth century.

African American Christianity is the story of a faith intended to suppress and oppress—transformed by God who came to set people free. When Joseph confronted his brothers in Egypt, he declared, "You meant evil against me; but God meant it for good" (Gen 50:20). "Go, Tell It on the Mountain" is testimony to God's power to confound human intentions and achieve divine purposes. Singing it today is a miracle—that it was composed at all and that it can be sung by all—both white and black:

> Go, tell it on the mountain,
> Over the hills and everywhere;
> Go, tell it on the mountain
> That Jesus Christ is born.

MEDITATION

Behind the Ranges

> Something hidden. Go and find it. Go and look behind the ranges—
> Something lost behind the Ranges. Lost and waiting for you. Go!

During my late teens some older friends gave me a book that used this line from Kipling's *The Explorer* as its title. It was a book about James Outram Fraser (1886–1938), a British Protestant missionary to China. Such a book was given, I'm fairly sure, to keep me "on track" toward a career as what we then termed a "foreign missionary." Being such a missionary was the main agenda in that church where, after my mostly churchless childhood, I came to faith. This church's reason for being was to "go tell it . . . everywhere." The mission outreach budget of the church exceeded the current expense budget, reflecting priorities that all churches would do well to emulate.

Many of my older friends became missionaries to Africa, Latin America, even Iran and Afghanistan. "Far, far away, in heathen darkness dwelling, millions of souls forever may be lost," we would sing heartily at the Wednesday evening prayer meeting. Later in life I would learn that many overseas missionaries did not share this dark vision of "lostness," but came to respect the religion and culture of those with whom they shared the good news. Indeed, many became a source of comfort, bringing education, medical care, and democracy to countries that eventually broke with their colonial masters. Those who went from our church, however, did not share that broader sympathy. Still, even though their doctrines were rejected by those of other faiths, I am sure that without realizing it, the sincere devotion of their lives must have reflected a genuine and practical love like that of Jesus who "went about doing good."

To prepare me for a missionary career, the pastor assigned a retired missionary to China the task of teaching me New Testament Greek—and I was only seventeen. This was to prepare me, perhaps, for work as a missionary translator. I did not become such a missionary, but I did go on to college and majored in classical Greek, a very useful tool in what became my life's work as a preacher. My debt to those good people is immense for equipping me for serious pulpit work.

There was, however, one major blind spot in the vision of that missionary-minded church. Those faithful folk lived and gave sacrificially to "tell it everywhere"—but not quite everywhere. Within a few short blocks of our downtown location there were low-income African American neighbors; however, we never reached out to them. "Those people have their own churches," I was told by an officer of the church when he learned that I had actually invited a "negro" prisoner, upon his release from the county jail, to worship at our church. The prisoner, Barney, never showed up at the place where I had promised to meet him; he surely must have known that my sincere invitation would not be matched by a similarly sincere welcome at a white church. All of this happened in the 1940s, and such a blind spot afflicted the vision of even "liberal" congregations in those days before Martin Luther King Jr. appeared on the scene.

What is interesting about the ministry of Jesus is that he seemed to go out of his way to go everywhere—anytime, anywhere, and everywhere his enemies didn't want him to go. He not only went to the lepers but even touched them, making himself ritually unclean. Likewise, he went to the disabled who, for no fault of their own, and because of their disabilities, were excluded from the temple (2 Sam 5:8), and could never enter the priesthood. Worse yet, he connected with Gentiles, an enemy Roman military officer, and with traitorous publicans who were tax collectors for the Romans. He did not shun a woman who was ritually unclean; he even talked with a half-breed Samaritan woman, and responded to the request of a Gentile, Syrophoenician woman. And to make it even more galling to the religious hierarchy, he deliberately did much of his healing, helping work on the Sabbath, as though to increase tensions with the exclusive religious establishment.

One of the hymnals my coauthor and I are using as we write this book places this carol on the page next to another carol, "Good Christian Friends, Rejoice" (pp. 44–50) so that as we open our hymnals we see both carols side-by-side. Reflecting upon Jesus' willingness to go anywhere, anytime, and everywhere to do God's healing work, it was certainly a wise and scriptural revision in wording when we began singing about Christian "friends," rather than Christian "men." Jesus called everyone a friend. Do we?

Every so often, I skip morning worship with my proper Presbyterian friends and steal away for silent worship with the Quakers, the Society of Friends. I wish that all of our churches could make that name the subtitle on our outdoor church bulletin boards. It would be wonderful to see a church sign that read, "First Presbyterian Church, A Society of Friends."

It's not easy these days to be a friend to everybody. It's not even easy in my little neighborhood where people want me to "take sides" on this or that issue. It's not easy to be friendly with everyone in a world where we're afraid of the bad guys, whether it's their bad, murderous actions, or what we define as their bad religion. But I simply cannot follow Jesus and call any of his friends (which includes everyone) anything other than my friends also.

Good Christian Friends, Rejoice

1 Good Chris-tian friends, re - joice with heart and soul and voice;
2 Good Chris-tian friends, re - joice with heart and soul and voice;
3 Good Chris-tian friends, re - joice with heart and soul and voice;

give ye heed to what we say: Je - sus Christ is born to - day;
now ye hear of end - less bliss; Je - sus Christ was born for this;
now ye need not fear the grave; Je - sus Christ was born to save;

ox and ass be - fore him bow, and he is in the man - ger now.
he has o - pened heav-en's door, and we are blest for - ev - er-more.
calls you one and calls you all to gain his ev - er - last - ing hall.

Christ is born to - day! Christ is born to - day!
Christ was born for this! Christ was born for this!
Christ was born to save! Christ was born to save!

Good Christian Friends, Rejoice

About the title of this carol: I grew up singing, "Good Christian Men, Rejoice," including "News! News!" and "Joy, Joy!" and "Peace, Peace!" after the third line. Hymnologists discovered that the exclamations don't belong in the hymn because they were based on a mistake by the tune's editor during the nineteenth century. By the late twentieth century, those words were dropped in most hymnbooks with virtually no controversy.

But "Good Christian Men" is another matter, for changing it to "Good Christian Friends" was part of the often acrimonious movement toward inclusive language, which began in the 1960s and 1970s. I was an advocate of that change. Led by my close friend and mentor, Hugh T. Kerr, the editor of *Theology Today*, we began making quiet changes in the journal's articles to reflect the concern that both men and women should be addressed—especially by the truth of the Christian faith. Most of the time the authors never noticed the alterations, but we discovered that when they did try to write in inclusive language, the result was often turgid and clumsy. So, in 1978 in *Theology Today* I published a little three-page guide to writing gracefully with inclusive language. It became the most widely circulated piece I have ever written.

The year 1978 also marked the first publication of "Good Christian Friends" in a Lutheran hymnbook. Since then, that is how the carol almost universally appears. I record all that history because it demonstrates two things. First, language changes. Second, as is evident in virtually every carol in this book, the music and words of Christmas carols are not sacrosanct. They are altered repeatedly over time, nearly always to good effect. After all, who would want to sing "Hark! How all the welkin rings," which is the way Charles Wesley wrote "Hark! The Herald Angels Sing" (pp. 52–57)?

The story behind "Good Christian Friends" is an example of musical mutations over time. Its origins are delightful. If the author of the hymn is to be believed, it literally came from heaven.

It was called "In Dulce Jubilo," and angels are said to have taught it to the German monk and mystic Heinrich Suso (c. 1295–1366). Suso wrote an autobiography, in which he refers to himself in the third person as "the Servant," and here is part of what he wrote about how he wrote this memorable carol:

"After he [Suso] had spent many hours in contemplating the joys of the angels and daybreak was at hand, there came to him a youth, who bore himself as though he were a heavenly musician sent to him by God; and with the youth came many other noble youths. . . . Now this same angel came up to the Servant right blithely, and said that God had sent him down to him, to bring him heavenly joys amid his sufferings; adding that he must cast off all his sorrows from his mind and bear them company, and that he must also dance with them in heavenly fashion.

"Then they drew the Servant by the hand into the dance, and the youth began a joyous song about the infant Jesus, which runs thus: 'In dulci jubilo,' etc. When the Servant heard the beloved name of Jesus sounding thus so sweetly, he became so joyful in his heart and feeling that the very memory of his sufferings vanished.

"It was a joy to him to see how exceedingly loftily and freely they bounded in the dance. . . . This dance was not of the kind that are danced on earth, but it was a heavenly movement, swelling up and falling back again into the wild abyss of God's hiddenness" (*The New Oxford Book of Carols* [1992]).

With changes and additions, "In Dulci Jubilo" was first published in a Lutheran hymnbook in 1533 that eliminated the last verse, which began, "Mater et filia," because that was too Catholic. In 1545 another version, with changes possibly made by Martin Luther, appeared in a Lutheran hymnbook. As *The New Oxford Book of Carols* succinctly notes, "Countless other [versions] followed."

The carol first appeared in English in 1853 as a very loose translation by John Mason Neale (1818–1866), one of the greatest contributors to our hymnody and a remarkable Christian pastor and scholar. Neale was a leader of a reform effort in the Church of England known as the Oxford Movement. It sought to return the church to some of its early and medieval roots, and because it drew its inspiration from the Orthodox and Roman Catholic traditions (in other words its Greek and Latin literature), it was very controversial. Yet Neale and a few others are almost solely responsible for bringing the richness of early and medieval Christianity into the modern church through their musical scholarship.

Neale's parents were ardent evangelicals, and their son was educated at Trinity College, Cambridge, and Downing College, where he excelled in all the disciplines—except mathematics. He eventually mastered twenty languages.

Because of the opposition of his superiors in the church and his severe lung problems, he spent almost his entire ministry as the warden of Sackville College, East Grinstead, London, which was actually a rescue mission for impoverished old men. Neale was the chaplain and survived on a miniscule salary of twenty-seven pounds annually. He was also one of the founders of an Anglican order the Sisterhood of St. Margaret's, which did pioneering work among women and children. He asked that his tombstone display this simple inscription (in Latin): "J. M. Neale, poor and unworthy priest resting under the sign of the cross."

Because of this sickly and impoverished pastor who ministered to the poor, we have today some of our greatest hymns, including "All Glory Laud and Honor," "Christ Is Made the Sure Foundation," "Come, Ye Faithful, Raise the Strain," "The Day of Resurrection," and, of course, "Good Christian Friends, Rejoice." In the Episcopal *Hymnal 1982*, there are forty-five hymns that in one way or another bear Neale's name—either as the author or as the translator.

One more historical note: On September 14, 1745, at a Moravian mission in Bethlehem, Pennsylvania, this carol was sung *simultaneously* in thirteen languages—European and Native American. It must have been a virtual Pentecost of Christmas piety, recalling the words of the inspiring Lenten hymn, "O Sacred Head Now Wounded": "What language can I borrow, to thank thee dearest Friend?"

MEDITATION

The Church of the Open Door

Well, that's what the sign said in front of the church, and I really liked that, so I thought I'd do some checking. Most church folks like to "sell" their church to a possible prospect, especially when it has an inviting name like that one, so I decided to ask some questions. It wasn't during the Christmas season when I made my inquiry, but it wasn't long before I wondered if they ever included the carol, "Good Christian Friends, Rejoice," in holiday worship. If they did, they evidently overlooked the words, "He hath opened Heaven's door." The architecture of the church building was modern, inviting, and open, but what impressed me most was that this assembly of true believers (as they called themselves) was constructed in such a way as to have an invisible architecture of exclusion.

The members did not realize how the unseen, but real, practice of this church resembled the architecture of the temple in Jesus' day. What do I mean? The edifice that Jesus cleansed (leading to his execution) had a set of physical concentric circles that defined who was "holier than thou." At the very center was the holy of holies into which the high priest could enter on only one day of the year. Next came a "court" into which only priests and Levites could enter. Next to that, ordinary Jewish laymen had their own court, and next to that, as you've already guessed, Jewish women had their own outer courtyard from which even they were excluded during menstruation.

Outside this last courtyard was a "no trespassing" sign, warning non-Jews that entrance was strictly prohibited—indeed, punishable by death. And worse yet, the temple's spiritual architecture communicated an even harsher cruelty; even Jews who were lame and disabled were disqualified from entry. We often miss the fact that the most significant "triumphal entry" on the first Palm Sunday was that of the blind and lame whom Jesus healed, thus allowing them to enter the temple from which, otherwise, they were excluded because of their disability.

Did the members of this "Church of the Open Door" realize that they had copied the temple of Jerusalem in the invisible spiritual design of their congregational life? It didn't take long to discover that this was not an open church. Not all members were full members, because only men could serve as church officers; women were second-class citizens, deprived of full participation in leadership. Then too, there was a certain orthodox way in which the Bible was interpreted; Scripture was forced into a certain creedal corral by the selection of proof texts that resulted in making the Bible say things that it really didn't say. There were also the right words with which one testified to one's faith; certain doctrinal shibboleths made it clear whether or not one was truly saved. Because of this, even though the outdoor sign had a subtitle, "All Are Welcome," it was clear that all were not welcome. There was an unwritten dress code, especially for the women, who didn't wear lipstick and had their hair piled high upon their heads in the accepted style.

Of course, the Church of the Open Door was nothing other than an exaggerated image of what has always existed in many respectable, mainline churches. We've all had ways of making the church something less than "a house of prayer for all peoples," which was why Jesus had to cleanse the temple of his day. There are still large denominations in which women may not serve as officers. Even though our seminaries educate women for the ministry, everyone knows there is not a level playing field when women seek their first call to a congregation. And racial minorities are still not welcomed with genuine enthusiasm in many congregations.

Many churches still have a physical architecture that limits the entrance and access of persons in wheelchairs (just try sitting in a wheelchair and opening the restroom doors in the average church facility). Divorced persons (especially clergy) have not always (and still are not) fully accepted in many churches. And then there's the big issue, sexual orientation, for which many sincere Christians are excluded or shunned. We have all found ways to keep all sorts of people on the sidelines of the church's life. When we're insiders, we fail to see how the church's message to many people has been, "Sorry, you can't play with us."

Mike Chimes was a deacon in the second church that I served. As a poor kid in the nearby Bronx, he had found a discarded harmonica in the gutter and had taught himself to make music with it—indeed, to make a whole life for himself on the harmonica. He moved on to better instruments over the years, playing on the vaudeville stage with the famed "Harmonica Rascals." Teaching his three sons to play, they became "The Musical Chimes," playing on such stages as New York's Palace Theatre. His little instrument provided the background accompaniment for Jackie Kennedy's tour of the White House, and his special licks can be heard on recordings of Frank Sinatra, Neil Diamond, Harry Belafonte, Pete Seeger, and Gladys Knight. Gaining such international recognition, he worked with the Hohner Company of Germany in the development of the larger chord harmonicas.

There was just one problem with Mike's artistry: he played the harmonica backwards, with the bass notes on the right rather than on the left. When he found that first harmonica in the gutter, the face plates were missing so that as he taught himself to play, he always held the harmonica upside down—and he never changed his backward, upside-down way of playing! But does it really matter? As Duke Ellington said, "If it sounds good, it is good."

Underneath all outward appearances, we're all very different from one another. We all play the game of life differently, but if we seek sincerely to follow Jesus, does it matter if my way of playing is unlike yours? After all, who really belongs to Jesus? He made it very clear one day when he said, "Whoever does the will of God is my brother and sister and mother" (Mark 3:35). That's the real family of God. So I say, "Just play it! If it sounds good to Jesus, it must surely be good!"

Hark! The Herald Angels Sing

1 Hark! the her-ald an-gels sing, "Glo-ry to the new-born King:
2 Christ, by high-est heaven a-dored, Christ, the ev-er-last-ing Lord,
3 Hail the heaven-born Prince of Peace! Hail the Sun of Right-eous-ness!

peace on earth, and mer-cy mild, God and sin-ners rec-on-ciled!"
late in time be-hold him come, off-spring of the Vir-gin's womb:
Light and life to all he brings, risen with heal-ing in his wings.

Joy-ful, all ye na-tions, rise, join the tri-umph of the skies;
veiled in flesh the God-head see; hail th'in-car-nate De-i-ty,
Mild he lays his glo-ry by, born that we no more may die,

with th'an-gel-ic host pro-claim, "Christ is born in Beth-le-hem!"
pleased with us in flesh to dwell, Je-sus, our Em-man-u-el.
born to raise us from the earth, born to give us sec-ond birth.

Hark! the her-ald an-gels sing, "Glo-ry to the new-born King."

Hark! The Herald Angels Sing

People sing this carol in Christmas services throughout all the world. From the time of its composition in the eighteenth century, it has enjoyed unbroken popularity. John Julian, a renowned hymnologist, declared that it was one of the four greatest Christmas carols, and another declared it "perhaps the most popular English hymn in the world."

If you read or sing it carefully, you will find that "Hark! The Herald Angels Sing" is really a summation of the Christian faith. Erik Routley said about its author, Charles Wesley (1707–1788), that his "hymns were composed in order that men and women might sing their way, not only into experience, but also into knowledge; . . . and the ignorant might be led into truth by the gentle hand of melody and rhyme."

"Hark! The Herald Angels Sing" was written approximately a year after Charles Wesley's conversion in 1738 while his heart was still aflame. He was co-founder of Methodism with his brother John, and it was Charles who gave Methodism its expansive spirit and vitality. (For an account of Charles Wesley's remarkable life, see pp. 25–28.)

Despite its centrality to Christmas worship, "Hark, the Herald Angels Sing" has an amazing history that demonstrates the tangled way in which the words of authors and the tunes of composers are not sacred writ but are altered and adapted over time. Even now, whenever a new hymn book is introduced, people will invariably exclaim: "They changed the words!" or "They changed the tune!" It was ever thus.

In 1739 Wesley published his poem as a "Hymn for Christmas Day" in a collection edited by his brother John, *Hymns and Sacred Poems*. The opening lines were:

> Hark! How all the welkin [heaven] rings
> Glory to the King of Kings.

Enter George Whitefield (1714–1770)—the greatest preacher of the eighteenth century and the Wesleys' theological opponent. He had an amazing gift for communicating to the masses. Even though the word "welkin" was still in use, he changed the beginning in his own hymnbook of 1754 and gave us the words that bring Christmas to life today:

> Hark, the herald angels sing,
> Glory to the new-born King.

This free-wheeling editing went on all the time, driving Charles Wesley to fulminate: "Many Gentlemen have done my Brother and me (though not without naming us) the honour to reprint many of our hymns. Now they are perfectly welcome to do so, provided they print them just as they are. But I desire they would not attempt to mend them—for they really are not able." Wesley went on to suggest archly that the poetic interlopers could take the minimal step of putting the original words in the margin so "that we may no longer be held responsible either for the nonsense or the doggerel of other men."

Charles Wesley's brother John was hardly above altering texts himself. He changed the beginning of Isaac Watts' great hymn from "Our God and help in ages past" to "O God, our help in ages past." Charles Wesley's complaints were ignored, and the wars over words ranged on. Occasionally the original composers were left unmentioned in the hymnbooks of others. Rarely were they consulted. Obviously, there were no copyright laws. The fact is that over time, Charles Wesley also changed his hymns, including "Hark! The Herald Angels Sing." From the nineteenth to the twenty-first century, other editors weighed in as well, and "Hark! The Herald Angels Sing" has been sung to various texts. Hymns are often the hybrid of many hands, and here the result is magnificent.

Then there is the matter of the tune. Charles Wesley wanted "slow and solemn music" for this classic Christmas hymn. Various tunes were attached to the ever-changing words, but none of them seemed right. In 1840, almost exactly one hundred years after Wesley published his words, Felix Mendelssohn composed a cantata to celebrate the 400th anniversary of the Gutenberg printing press. Mendelssohn rather liked his "gay and popular" creation and thought of adapting the music to other uses, but he said the tune was "soldierlike and buxom" and believed "it will never do to [use] sacred words." Shortly after, young English organist W. H. Cummings took Mendelssohn's music and adapted it to "Hark! The Herald Angels Sing," and, with some changes, that is what we sing today.

The editors of the authoritative *Oxford Book of Carols* have declared that Wesley's hymn was "a poem in search of a melody. Mendelssohn's music, on the other hand, was a melody in search of a poem." Another historian has concluded, "The process that brought them together is one of those happy accidents that bestride the history of hymnody."

Or, perhaps the creation of "Hark! The Herald Angels Sing" is an example of the profound paradox of God's revelation in Jesus Christ—the boy who was born a king, an unseen God who became flesh and dwelt among us, divine power sacrificed so that we might live. Wesley's and Mendelssohn's plans and expectations were confounded in history, and the result is pure paradoxical beauty.

> Mild he lays his glory by,
> Born that we no more may die.

May it be so for everyone. May all our intentions and desires be transformed by Christ for the redemption of others, for certainly "the hopes and fears of all the years are met in Thee tonight."

MEDITATION

Veiled in Flesh

Yes, it's all about paradox, as my coauthor states. And we'll never grasp the revolutionary message of Christianity unless we can live with paradox, particularly the paradox that God once enjoyed life in a human body. "Please," someone says, "let's be reverent and not talk about God having a good time in a physical body." According to some devout souls, we're not supposed to be shamelessly enjoying our bodily life. After all, aren't we awaiting our day of release when, at last, having exited our mortal body ("shuffled off this mortal coil," as in Shakespeare's *Hamlet*), we'll make our escape to heaven? In that gospel hymn, "Sweet Hour of Prayer," that's the transcendent hope of which we sing, "This robe of flesh I'll drop, and rise to seize the everlasting prize."

Sorry, but that's not the good news that was proclaimed when Paul carried the message of Jesus into the Greco-Roman world. For that matter, the hope of escaping our bodily life and ascending to a nonphysical realm was exactly what that Gentile world *already* believed. The "Gospel according to Plato" (and other similar philosophers) viewed our physical body as a temporary container from which we will finally escape so that we can rise to the real world of the spirit.

Paul's sermon in Athens (Acts 17:22–34) got off to a good start when his opening words echoed the very first words of Plato's *Apology*, "Men of Athens" (*andres Athenaioi*), and he continued to charm his audience by quoting one of their poets. However, it all went sour, and his audience "scoffed" when he mentioned the resurrection of the body. This bodily stuff was exactly what they didn't want to hear. After all, once we disconnect spirit from body, anything goes. Because there's no connection, I can do whatever I want with my body, or with the bodies of others. Slavery is okay because it's someone else's body. I can sleep with anyone who satisfies my sexual appetites because there's no spiritual connection or damage. I can abuse the bodies of animals—or the physical earth and its environment—because it's all just vile, physical stuff.

In glaring contrast to this alienation from the body, early Christianity was alarmingly physical. In Jesus Christ, God became physical, and so we sing "Veiled in flesh, the Godhead see." The worship of the first Christians, in which they ate actual bread and drank real wine, was too crudely physical to sophisticated Greeks and Romans who worshiped ideas and ideals. Those early Christians actually called themselves "the body of Christ." How revolting that must have been to people who hoped to escape their bodies.

Christians talked about a physically empty tomb, of a risen One who broke bread with them, cooked breakfast for them on the shores of the Sea of Tiberias, and even said, "Touch me and see; for a ghost does not have flesh and bones as you see that I have." It was all too disgustingly physical to the sophisticated Greco-Roman world.

Those Christians believed that it was going to get even better. They insisted that we were going to get a better body like the risen body of Jesus and live on a newly restored earth. We still talk that way today at gravesides when the officiant offers a committal prayer, speaking of our risen Lord "at whose coming in glorious majesty the earth and the sea shall give up their dead; and the mortal bodies of those who sleep in Him shall be raised, and changed, and made like unto His own glorious body."

So it does matter that we treat our bodies with reverence because the same paradox—the same mystical union of body and spirit—has happened to us. Our bodies are temples of the Holy Spirit, just as the body of Jesus was a spiritual unity of humanity and divinity. It does matter with whom we sleep and make love—genuine, committed love. It does matter that we care for our bodies, eat nourishing food in proper amounts, and receive sufficient rest and exercise. And it matters, especially, that we see to it that the bodies of others receive the same reverent care and attention. Preaching a gospel of words is meaningless, unless we preach the full gospel, a gospel full of food, clothing, shelter, and justice—especially for those who languish in our miserable prison systems. It all matters, because we see God "veiled in flesh."

After we've begun to see these things correctly, then it will be time to have real fun, because I suspect that someday we'll arrive at the startling truth that Jesus really did have fun, really did enjoy "the days of his flesh," his bodily years on earth. Listen to these words from G. K. Chesterton as he comes to the heart of his faith in Jesus: "I say it with reverence—there was in that shattering personality a thread that must be called shyness. There was something that He hid from all men when He went up a mountain to pray. There was something that He covered constantly by abrupt silence or impetuous isolation. There was some one thing that was too great for God to show us when He walked upon our earth, and I have sometimes fancied that it was His mirth."

I Wonder as I Wander

1 I won - der as I wan - der, out un - der the sky, how
2 When Ma - ry birthed Je - sus, 'twas in a cow's stall, with
3 If Je - sus had want - ed for an - y wee thing, a
4 I won - der as I wan - der, out un - der the sky, how

Je - sus the Sav - ior did come for to die for
wise men and farm - ers and shep - herds and all, but
star in the sky or a bird on the wing, or
Je - sus the Sav - ior did come for to die for

poor ordi - nary peo - ple like you and like I; I
high from God's heav - en a star's light did fall, the
all of God's an - gels in heaven for to sing, he
poor ordi - nary peo - ple like you and like I; I

won - der as I wan - der, out un - der the sky.
prom - ise of a - ges it then did re - call.
sure - ly could have it, 'cause he was the King.
won - der as I wan - der, out un - der the sky. Out un - der the sky.

I Wonder as I Wander

This carol doesn't appear in many hymnbooks. In fact, according to the authoritative hymnary.org, it has been published in only twelve English-language hymnals, compared to 504 for "Silent Night." One reason may be that it didn't appear until the twentieth century, so it has yet to find a large following. Another may be that it is a folk carol, emerging out of the Appalachian mountains.

It was "written" or "collected" by John Jacob Niles (1892–1980), the famous Kentucky folklorist and singer. The date was July 16, 1933; the place was the town of Murphy in the Appalachian mountains of North Carolina. Niles was attending a fundraising meeting organized by evangelicals who had been run out of town by the police.

Here is how he recalled the moment he heard the song for the first time: "A girl had stepped out to the edge of the little platform attached to the automobile. She began to sing. Her clothes were unbelievably dirty and ragged, and she, too, was unwashed. Her ash-blond hair hung down in long skeins, uncombed. . . . But, best of all, she was positively beautiful, and in her untutored way, she could sing. She smiled as she sang, smiled rather sadly, and sang only a single line of a song."

Niles was captivated. He persuaded the girl, Annie Morgan, to sing the fragment eight times for a quarter each time she sang. Afterwards, she became suspicious, disappeared into the countryside, and was lost in history. It's unclear whether Niles heard only one line or three lines, but he knew he had found "a garbled fragment of melodic material—and a magnificent idea."

He expanded the melody to four lines and the lyrics to three stanzas, completing his work on October 4, 1933. Niles performed "I Wonder as I Wander" for the first time on December 19, 1933, at the John C. Campbell Folk School in Brasstown, North Carolina and published it in *Songs of the Hill Folk* (1934). Later, he had to file lawsuits about "I Wonder as I Wander" because some considered the Christmas song to be anonymous, so the legacy of this carol became as tangled as its mysterious origin.

During the 1950s and 1960s, Niles was a major force in the twentieth-century revival of American folk music among many singers, including Joan Baez, Burl Ives, and Peter, Paul, and Mary. Born in Louisville, Kentucky, he began collecting Appalachian folk songs from Eastern Kentucky as a traveling salesman from 1910 to 1917. After World War I, he received classical music training in France and the United States and sang opera and then folk songs in the early days of radio. During the 1920s and 1930s he performed both classical and folk music in Europe and the United States and sang at the White House in 1938.

Folk music from both the white and African American traditions was his passion. At only the age of sixteen, he composed "Go 'Way From My Window," which he eventually published in 1930. Marlene Dietrich recorded it, and Bob Dylan used it as the initial line of "It Ain't Me Babe." He is responsible for composing or arranging more than one-hundred folk songs, including "Black Is the Color of My True Love's Hair" and "Jesus, Jesus, Rest Your Head." For decades he lived with his wife on a farm in Kentucky, and toward the end of his life he returned to more classical works, including a composition using poems by his close friend and fellow Kentuckian, Thomas Merton.

"I Wonder as I Wander" is perhaps more often performed than sung by congregations. Many artists have recorded the song; several composers have made arrangements of it, including Benjamin Britten and John Rutter in England. The African American poet Langston Hughes used it for the title of his autobiography.

Whenever and wherever it is sung, it never escapes its inception on the lips of an impoverished blonde girl, singing in the mountains, "I Wonder as I Wander." Historian William E. Studwell has described it as "absolutely haunting and esthetically chilling when sung by a suitable high soprano" and "decidedly spiritual in tone and ethereal in sensation."

For those who have less than total certainty about their faith, for those who ponder the mystery of Christmas with uneasiness and awe, "I Wonder as I Wander" speaks powerfully about "how Jesus the Savior did come for to die/for poor ordinary people like you and like I." It is a song for all of us who wonder as we wander, out under the sky.

MEDITATION

A Wanderer's Way

It's a very long way from Louisville, Kentucky, birthplace of Appalachian balladeer John Jacob Niles, to the halls of learning at Christ's College, Cambridge, in England. However, as soon as we decided to include this song of Niles's in our collection, I realized that the two places were forever connected in my mind.

One of the most memorable mornings of my life took place in the 1960s when our small group of ministers spent the entire morning picking the brains of Canon Charles E. Raven, formerly canon of Liverpool Cathedral, Regius Professor of Divinity at Cambridge, and Master of Christ's College Cambridge. Canon Raven was speaking in New York City, and one of our group invited him to make the short train trip to Mount Vernon, New York, to spend a morning with us.

A scholar of immense learning, the product of a traditional British education in the classics, Raven could read Greek and Latin with the ease with which we read English. He was steeped particularly in patristic theology (the Greek and Latin early church fathers), but his boundless curiosity had carried him into the realms of biology and psychology. As a result, a major contribution of his life was to annul the divorce which should never have occurred between religion and science. As a young pastor, I was "blown away" by the breadth and depth of his mind. How does one accumulate so much learning in a lifetime?

But there was something else. At the end of that morning, I came away somehow touched by what I can only call a vibrant spiritual presence. It was not only a great mind to which I had been exposed; here too was also a great, all-embracing heart. I just couldn't "name it."

But then, many years later, in November 2002, I came upon a book in the Louisville Seminary Library written by Canon Raven (British edition 1928, American edition 1929). For some reason, I had been unaware that he had written such a book relatively early in his career, a story of his spiritual journey "up to that date." It was entitled *A Wander's Way*, and I have kept both editions near me ever since.

I would never have thought of Charles Raven as a "wanderer," but much of his life's story is that of a wondering, wandering soul. As a student, he arrived at Cambridge in the early 1900s as a self-confessed "pure pagan," assuming that he would follow his father's profession as a barrister. However, his lifelong love of being in the forests, especially as a collector of *Lepidoptera* (moths), led to a kind of "conversion" in which he sensed that beyond the beauty and glory of nature was a Being "loving and good."

Still, he had no firm plan of entering the ministry, and so, upon the completion of his studies, he took a position as assistant secretary for secondary education under the Liverpool county council, during which he wandered on to another "road less traveled." At the invitation of a fellow worker, he began helping at a boys' club that met in a slum warehouse. Ministering to poor waifs, he said, "the odour was like that of an Irish cattle-boat in a rough sea." Still, God came nearer to him amidst those street urchins than in any cathedral. What an odd wanderer he was, experiencing heaven in the smelly air of children's poverty, while on other nights studying the arcane subtleties of the fourth-century Apollinarian heresy.

At that same time, he went to visit a friend who was ill but had "found Jesus." His friend made no attempt to convert him; indeed, they talked mostly of old times, old friends, and old books, but one thing was clear: "a third person was there." This day spent with his old friend became a turning point. The Jesus who had survived death and appeared to his first friends was alive and with us still today. Raven's life, thereafter, became an adventure in finding Jesus, not only in the expected ecclesiastical places, but whenever and wherever life was being lived and things were being done in a Christlike spirit. It was a sense of Jesus' presence that never deserted him. He faced imminent death three times as a chaplain on the Western Front during World War I, but his assurance of the presence of Jesus remained unshaken. That was the spiritual presence I could not describe on that morning back in the 1960s.

My copy of *A Wanderer's Way* has probably more pencil markings in it than any other book in my library, and since discovering it, I have encountered fellow sojourners who live with that same sense of the presence of the living and risen Jesus. In their differing ways of life they have taught me the importance of a life of wondering and wandering, and of how Jesus can be found in the most unexpected persons and places, in what I was sure was the "wrong" person, church, or religion. All of a sudden, he's undeniably present, defying all my neat definitions. So I try to remember every morning that I just may meet Jesus today. Thomas Merton has given us the best prayer for beginning every day:

My Lord God, I have no idea where I am going. I do not see the road ahead of me. I cannot know for certain where it will end. Nor do I really know myself, and the fact that I think that I am following your will does not mean that I am actually doing so. But I believe that the desire to please you does in fact please you. And I hope I have that desire in all that I am doing. I hope that I will never do anything apart from that desire. And I know that if I do this you will lead me by the right road though I may know nothing about it. Therefore will I trust you always though I may seem to be lost and in the shadow of death. I will not fear, for you are ever with me, and you will never leave me to face my perils alone (*Thoughts in Solitude*).

In the Bleak Mid-Winter

1 In the bleak mid - win - ter, frost - y wind made moan,
2 Our God, heaven can - not hold him, nor earth sus - tain;
3 An - gels and arch - an - gels may have gath - ered there,
4 What can I give him, poor as I am?

earth stood hard as i - ron, wa - ter like a stone;
heaven and earth shall flee a - way when he comes to reign:
cher - u - bim and ser - a - phim thronged the air;
If I were a shep - herd, I would bring a lamb;

snow had fall - en, snow on snow, snow on snow,
in the bleak mid - win - ter a sta - ble - place suf - ficed
but his moth - er on - ly, in her maid - en bliss,
if I were a wise man, I would do my part;

in the bleak mid - win - ter, long a - go.
the Lord God in - car - nate, Je - sus Christ.
wor - shiped the Be - lov - ed with a kiss.
yet what I can I give him: give my heart.

In the Bleak Mid-Winter

Christina Georgina Rossetti (1830–1894) was a Christian mystic and brilliant poet. Her spiritual and aesthetic genius came from her family. Her father was an Italian refugee from the authoritarian government in Naples and became a poet and professor at King's College, London. Her mother was a devout Anglo-Catholic and deeply influenced Christina's piety. Her brother, Dante Gabriel Rossetti, also wrote poetry but achieved lasting recognition as a pre-Raphaelite painter. Christina herself was "strikingly beautiful," and she became a model for her brother and his painter friends.

With beauty within and all around her, why then "In the Bleak Mid-Winter"? The answer seems to lie in her severe, ascetic spirituality, accentuated by frail health. Even as she lay dying, she asked that her church pray for her but not use her name. She refused two offers of matrimony for religious reasons; one of them came from a man she deeply loved. She apparently believed that if she longed for God, she could not belong to another.

The powerful Romantic movement of the nineteenth century bleeds through the lines of "In the Bleak Mid-Winter," but the carol cannot be understood without understanding the heart of Christian mysticism—the quest to be at one with God. Christina Rossetti understood that journey and embodied it.

Rossetti crafted "In the Bleak Mid-Winter" as a poem, not a carol, which explains why it is somewhat difficult to sing. Like other poets and artists, she gave her Christmas a contemporary setting amidst the harsh winter of England, rather than warmer Palestine. Her poem, one of four Christmas works, was composed sometime before it was first published in 1872, and then it appeared in her posthumous *Poetical Works* (1904). It became popular when Gustav Holst provided the gorgeous melody, "Cranham," and "In the Bleak Mid-Winter" made its Christmas debut in *The English Hymnal* of 1906.

Holst (1874–1934) was an excellent teacher and one of the finest composers of the twentieth century. Afflicted with defective eyes and neuritis and frustrated in realizing his dream of becoming a concert pianist, he turned to the trombone as his instrument and displayed a heroic spirit in the midst of adversity. One friend told him, "I feel that the evil and scandal in the world must put its tail between its legs when it meets you." A lifelong friend of Ralph Vaughn Williams, Holst held prestigious teaching and music appointments on both sides of the Atlantic, and in 1916 he composed his masterpiece, "The Planets." He inherited his musical passion across three generations, and it was contagious. He had, according to one observer, the capacity "from his village days, of communicating a love for the finest music to any body of men, women or children with whom he might happen to meet." Humbled by his own limitations, he was known to advise others: "A little learning is *not* a dangerous thing, as long as you know that it is only a little."

The setting of this carol is, of course, winter, and here a bit of history might be helpful in understanding Rossetti's poem. We don't know the date of Christ's birth. December 25 was finally set as the day for Christmas in the fourth century when the church absorbed the pagan festivals of the midwinter solstice and Christianized the celebrations. Although not unheard of, snow in Palestine is rare. John Milton's "On the Morning of Christ's Nativity," composed in 1629, greatly influenced the English connection between snow and Christmas. But when Charles Dickens issued *A Christmas Carol* in 1843, a snowy Christmas became a fixture of the imagination of the English-speaking world—whether there was or could even be snow on the ground. (For more background, see "Introduction," pp. xiii–xviii.)

The theology of "In the Bleak Mid-Winter" has been questioned. Ian Bradley, the author of *The Penguin Book of Carols,* has written, "Is it right to say that heaven cannot hold God, nor the earth sustain, and what about heaven and earth fleeing away when he comes to reign—earth perhaps, but is heaven going to flee at the second coming?" A worthy question perhaps but one ignorant of the biblical vision of John of Patmos: "Then I saw a new heaven and a new earth; for the first heaven and the first earth had passed away" (Rev 21:1). For Christina Rossetti, that was Christ's arrival at the end of time. Her mysticism made her yearn for the day when God "will wipe away every tear from their eyes, and death shall be no more, neither shall there be mourning nor crying nor pain any more, for the former things have passed away" (Rev 21:4).

Little wonder that she knelt before the manger in awe, asking the eternal question of Christmas for us all:

What can I give him, poor as I am?
If I were a shepherd, I would bring a lamb;
If I were a wise man, I would do my part;
Yet what can I give him: give him my heart.

MEDITATION

Oh, Look, It's Snowing!

We wonder why poet Christina Rossetti located Jesus' birth "in the bleak midwinter." Nothing in Scripture tells us that "snow on snow" had fallen at that time; we are not even told that baby Jesus arrived during winter. For that matter, millions of Christians in our world have never known a snowy Christmas. Still, the Victorian gospel according to Currier and Ives (and now Hallmark) has placed the nativity within sentimental scenes of winter in the countryside, with cozy gatherings around grandmother's fireplace, all of which can be a burden for those who find themselves alone during the holidays.

In her book, *At the Still Point*, Carol Buckley says that one of the most difficult times of the year for someone living alone is at the change of seasons when, for example, you wake up on a December morning, look out the window, and discover that the first snow of the season is blanketing the earth in silent whiteness. You start to say, "Oh, look, it's snowing!"—but there's no one there listening.

In the year I read that book, I was alone during the holidays. Walking through a shopping mall, I saw something that caught my attention. Near the food court, a singing Santa, with warbling organ accompaniment, was leading a group of parents and children in the syrupy ballad "Silver Bells," and how "it's Christmas time in the city." It was all quite "schmaltzy," not my thing, so I might have passed on had I not seen an elderly woman, dressed plainly, seated alone at a table under the escalator. With a Styrofoam coffee cup in front of her, she was happily singing along all by herself.

Now why did I stop to watch?

Preachers often need to be needed, so maybe I wanted to see if she was "all right." Did I expect her to start weeping, in need of my ministrations? But after all, what's so odd about being able to sing when one is alone, even if you're not part of the Christmas crowd? Is it some kind of failure to live alone—or to sing alone? She apparently didn't need my help, so I walked on and returned home to my own solitary apartment.

Alone by myself, beginning work on a sermon text, I suddenly realized that I had just seen an elderly, modern version of the Virgin Mary who, we are told, began singing alone, all by herself, when she learned that she was about to become a pregnant, unwed teenager. Now that's an amazing woman! We miss all of this because her song, "The Magnificat," has become such an elaborately performed piece of classical music at the holidays. In its scriptural setting, however, it's the solo of a young woman who is, of all women in her day, very much alone, but still singing!

Then I realized something about Mary and why she could sing. She was not alone; she was singing to the unborn God within her! The One whom John's gospel calls the Word was becoming flesh within her womb, within the life of Mary. The gift of real song is within—the grace of an inner presence. Mary's kind of singing cannot be taught; it is a gift of spiritual presence, and people who are possessed by that presence are never alone. Even if they can't "carry a tune in a bucket," people who sing like Mary can keep on singing, even in those times when others become whiners.

Does the great turning point in any life take place when we become aware of a presence within us that has always been there, waiting to be born, recognized? The really big miracle began when Mary opened her heart to the Child who was singing within her life. That's the real miraculous conception!

I don't know why that woman in the mall was able to sing her song. I don't know what she believed, what brand of Christianity she embraced, or if she even claimed to be a Christian. But all over the world you can find people who have discovered the light of that inner presence. And that discovery has made all the difference in their lives, even if they give that presence another name than the one we know.

Our world has been visited by a holy child who came to stay, to reside secretly in every life. He is "the true light, which enlightens everyone" (John 1:9). That child slipped silently into the heart of Mary when she heard a song being sung from somewhere deep within her and made a place for that child in her heart. Christina Rossetti brings her lovely carol to an end on that note: the one and only gift we can give to God is our heart. And that gift becomes a mutual indwelling as Christ lives not only in our heart, but as we live in God's heart. Our lives, as Paul wrote, are "hid with Christ in God" (Col 3:3). The God who became incarnate in the life of Jesus will always be present whenever we say, "Oh, look, it's snowing!"

It Came Upon the Midnight Clear

1 It came up-on the mid-night clear, that glo-rious song of old,
2 Still through the clo - ven skies they come, with peace-ful wings un - furled,
3 Yet with the woes of sin and strife the world has suf-fered long;
4 And you, be-neath life's crush-ing load, whose forms are bend-ing low,
5 For lo, the days are has-tening on, by proph-ets seen of old,

from an - gels bend - ing near the earth, to touch their harps of gold:
and still their heaven-ly mu - sic floats o'er all the wea - ry world:
be - neath the heaven-ly hymn have rolled two thou-sand years of wrong;
who toil a - long the climb - ing way with pain - ful steps and slow,
when with the ev - er - cir-cling years shall come the time fore - told,

"Peace on the earth, good will to all, from heaven's all-gra-cious King":
a - bove its sad and low - ly plains they bend on hov-ering wing,
and we at war on earth hear not the tid - ings that they bring;
look now, for glad and gold - en hours come swift - ly on the wing:
when peace shall o - ver all the earth its an - cient splen-dors fling,

the world in sol - emn still-ness lay, to hear the an - gels sing.
and ev - er o'er its Ba - bel sounds the bless-ed an - gels sing.
O, hush the noise and cease the strife to hear the an - gels sing!
O, rest be - side the wea - ry road, and hear the an - gels sing.
and the whole world give back the song which now the an - gels sing.

It Came Upon the Midnight Clear

Edmund Hamilton Sears (1810–1876) marched to a different drummer. As a boy growing up in Massachusetts, he loved poetry. He began writing his own verse at the age of ten, and and he walked around reciting his favorite poem, Alexander Pope's "Iliad." One of his ancestors was a Calvinist pilgrim, but he became a Unitarian—with a difference. "I believe and preach the divinity of Christ," he wrote just before he died. He studied for the ministry at Harvard Divinity School, but unlike his contemporaries he decided to serve small churches. "I had no other ambition than to lead such a quiet pastorate as Goldsmith describes in *The Deserted Village*," he declared.

He believed ardently in the spiritual power of music. "The song, or hymn," he declared, "should be a summing up of the sermon, helping us to take home its truth, and so carry it with us to fill our daily life with its melodies."

Like many writers in nineteenth-century America, he was utterly optimistic about the future, and like many of his Unitarian colleagues in ministry, he had a keen social conscience. This ethical perspective makes his poem, "It Came Upon the Midnight Clear," a different, but not unique, Christmas carol.

Sears wrote his memorable classic on a snowy day in December 1849 in the small town of Wayland, Massachusetts, where he had taken early retirement because of ill health. The Mexican-American War had just ended. Europe had been rocked by the revolutions of 1848. The United States was bitterly divided over slavery, and a civil war loomed. Sears's poem was immediately published and gained great popularity both in the United States and England. It was wedded in the United States to the tune "Carol," by Richard Storrs Willis (1819–1900). In England, the carol has been sung to the tune of "Noel."

The result was the first wholly American Christmas carol to achieve international fame, and today it ranks only behind "O Little Town of Bethlehem" in American carols with worldwide renown.

Even though the Unitarian Sears believed in Jesus as divine, there is nothing about Christ in his carol, except perhaps the reference to "heaven's all gracious King." The "it" of "It Came Upon the Midnight Clear" refers to "that glorious song of old," not the birth of Jesus. That led the English Reformed Church hymn expert, Erik Routley, to write acidly, "As we sing it, . . . the hymn is little more than an ethical song extolling the worth and splendor of peace among men." That hasn't stopped a broad range of Christians, from liberal and evangelical Protestants to Roman Catholics, from including it in an astonishing 717 hymnbooks. After all, Sears wrote it as "*the* Midnight clear," not "*a* Midnight clear," as a few variant versions have it.

Sears's carol is extremely important, for it marks the beginning of what are called "Social Gospel" hymns. There is no precise definition of what this genre is, but the Social Gospel hymns have grown in use and popularity from the nineteenth through the twenty-first century. Perhaps the best known is "O Master, Let Me Walk With Thee," written in 1879 by the "father of the Social Gospel," Washington Gladden (1836–1918), and published in 470 hymnals. Broadly understood, a Social Gospel hymn is simply one in which eternal truths are applied to temporal issues.

Sometimes, that isn't popular—in Sears's day or our own. "It Came Upon the Midnight Clear" has a lot of angels, but they don't hover placidly above the plain. Consider this verse:

> And you, beneath life's crushing load, whose forms are bending low,
> Who toil along the climbing way with painful steps and slow,
> Look now, for glad and golden hours come swiftly on the wing,
> O, rest beside the weary road, and hear the angels sing.

Perhaps "glad and golden hours" shimmers with nineteenth-century optimism, but there's another verse of prophetic power. Listen to Sears:

> Yet with the woes of sin and strife the world has suffered long;
> Beneath the heavenly hymn have rolled two thousand years of wrong;
> And we at war on earth hear not the tiding that they bring;
> O hush the noise and cease the strife to hear the angels sing.

"It Came Upon the Midnight Clear" may not be blatantly Christian, but it is Christlike. It celebrates the essence of Christian discipleship and looks to a future when the angels' glad tidings shall become a cosmic reality. Like the

Son of God, this carol surveys the world of want and war and offers a vision "when peace shall over all the earth its ancient splendors fling."

No wonder Christians around the world sing it. It's realistic—about what is and what will be.

MEDITATION

Comes Round the Age of Gold

In another meditation in this book I've mentioned the value of paradox, of learning to deal with some questions by answering, "Yes, but." So I'm asking, "Is the age of gold in some far away future, or are we already living in such a wonderland because of Jesus birth?" I remember Aunt Lottie at Christmastime, playing "Winter Wonderland" on her piano. There was always snow at the holidays in my northern town, and the snow made Christmas even more of an enchanted experience. But then, by sometime in late March, the snow would be mostly gone, and even long before that, the Christmas magic melted away. It's hard to hold on to Christmas.

Mrs. Magee, who lived across the street, tried to hold on to it by keeping her Christmas tree as long as possible. But then, by early February (I'm not making this up), out it would come, all dry and brown, a ghostlike skeleton. Even so, I still say "yes" to my question; I think the age of gold is already here, and that we're living right now in a Christmas wonderland.

In Frankenmuth, Michigan, it always seems like Christmas. At least, it has always seemed that way to me because of a special store in that town. Bronner's Christmas Wonderland is the largest Christmas store in the world. Just the building is over seven acres in size. Situated on twenty-seven acres of land, the parking lot accommodates 1,080 cars and fifty buses. Inside the Alpine-style building, some 100,000 lights illuminate the half-mile Christmas Lane. Except for closing on Christmas Day and Easter, it's always Christmas at Bronner's.

Maybe I'm crazy, but I'd really like to try working part-time at Bronner's. My guess is that the locals who find steady employment there would tell me that the glow of Christmas is hard to maintain on a year-round basis, but still I'd like to try, because I really believe that's the way it's meant to be for those of us who follow Jesus. Yes, I know that the New Testament takes us from the cradle to the cross, and that discipleship is not all sweetness and light, but I still think that we live in an enchanted world—in a Christmas wonderland.

As is made clear by other meditations in this book, the incarnation of God in Jesus Christ has revealed to us a heavenly Father who is unchangeably kind and gracious. The fearsome God who, in many primitive religions, was dreaded and placated with animal and even human sacrifices, was happily dismissed by the fearless, friendly God who came to us as a vulnerable baby. If that is what God is like, then we are already living in a universe of divine splendor, in the age of gold. In such a world, every person is as precious as a child on Christmas morning, a dear child of God, someone whom I can embrace as my friend.

"Hold it now," someone says, "You're getting carried away with all this Christmas stuff. Once a year is enough! There comes a time for tossing out the tree and putting the ornaments away." Well, yes, that's true. To my glowing "yes," there needs also to be a realistic "but then." Life can't be spiritually like a year-round Christmas store unless you work at keeping Christmas as an ever-present reality. Henry Van Dyke offered a long list of steps that any of us can take if we really want to keep Christmas. Just a few of them are worth quoting:

> Are you willing to forget what you have done for other people, and to remember what other people have done for you; to ignore what the world owes you, and to think what you owe the world; to put your rights in the background, and your duties in the middle distance, and your chances to do a little more than your duty in the foreground; to see that your fellow-men are just as real as you are, and try to look behind their faces to their hearts, hungry for joy; to own that probably the only good reason for your existence is not what you are going to get out of life, but what you are going to give to life; to close your book of complaints against the management of the universe, and look around you for a place where you can sow a few seeds of happiness—are you willing to do these things even for a day? Then you can keep Christmas . . . . And if you keep it for a day, why not always?

Recovering Christmas, which has been buried under an avalanche of acquisitiveness and cheapened by cleverly commercialized covetousness, will happen, as in all recovery programs, "one day at a time." If you can do it for just one day, that will be the best beginning. Do it for one day, then try another. It will begin to be your way of life, and you'll begin to be one of those angels of whom we sing, "still through the cloven skies they come, with peaceful wings unfurled." You won't sprout wings or gain any kind of halo; you'll just be you, the childlike you that somehow got lost along the way. But you'll be able to carry Christmas with you throughout the year.

I think I've been typing these simple words long enough to get my point across. Even though it's eighty-three degrees outside today, I think I'll slip a disk into my little CD player, and listen to "Winter Wonderland."

Joy to the World

Joy to the World

"Joy to the World" is the headliner of all the Christmas carols. It is the most-published Christmas hymn in North America, and it has been carried throughout the world in multiple translations. If you look at album recordings of Christmas carols, many will be called "Joy to the World" or it will be the first selection of the series.

Therefore, you may be shocked to find out that this famous Christmas carol wasn't intended for Christmas at all. "Joy to the World's" original title was "The Messiah's Coming and Kingdom." It was based on Psalm 98:4–9 and Christianized by Isaac Watts as a joyful celebration that Jesus Christ will return at the end of the world and draw the entire creation to salvation. And yet, no matter where you turn today, "Joy to the World" is a Christmas paean of praise for the beginning of Christ's life, not God's triumphal conclusion to history. It's always found in the section for Christmas in hymnals, and no Christmas will pass without carolers straining to hit its high notes and remain true to its lively rhythm.

It was written by Isaac Watts (1674–1748), often called "the father of English hymnody." Watts was simply a genius. With Charles Wesley, who succeeded him in time, he launched the golden age of English hymnody.

A word of background is needed about the times in which Watts did his work.

Until Watts, there was very little English hymnody. Because of the influence of English Puritans and Scotch Presbyterians, people sang the Psalms. Then came Watts, who wrote hymns.

A huge and violent argument broke out.

On the one hand, the psalm singers said that the only thing people should sing is the words of the Bible—specifically the Psalms.

On the other hand, Watts and others said that if you only sang the Psalms, you could not sing about Christ and the truth of the New Testament, including Jesus' birth. This didn't mean Watts and his cohort didn't like the Psalms. On the contrary, they often turned to the Psalms as the basis for their hymns—as with "Joy to the World," based on Psalm 98.

Watts's primary opponent, Thomas Bradbury, said Watts wrote "whims," not "hymns." Watts irenically replied, "I am fully persuaded that the Jewish psalm book was never designed to be the only Psalter for the Christian church."

One of Watts's contemporaries tells the story of visiting a friend, whose maid refused to join in the hymn-singing. She declared, "If you must know the plain truth, Sir, as long as you sung Jesus Christ's Psalms, I sung along with ye; but now that you sing Psalms of your own invention, ye may sing by yourselves."

Both sides had a point. But the argument was sometimes vicious and certainly prolonged. It lasted nearly half a century. It's striking that about every fifty to one-hundred years, there is a fight about music in the church. We saw it again in the nineteenth century when gospel hymns were introduced and then in the late twentieth and early twenty-first century with the rise of "contemporary Christian worship."

Basically, Watts and the hymn singers won the fight—decisively. The tradition of psalm singing was essentially obliterated from much of English-speaking worship, except in Scotland, and is only now staging a comeback.

To give you an idea of how bitter this fight was, even in America, consider the case of the Rev. Adam Rankin. In 1789 (more than fifty years after Watts's death), Rev. Rankin rode on horseback from his congregation in Kentucky to the first General Assembly of the Presbyterian Church in the United States of America.

He pleaded with his fellow Presbyterians "to refuse to allow the great and pernicious error of adopting the use of Watts' hymns in public worship in preference to Rouse's versifications of the Psalms of David." The General Assembly listened and, in a model of Christian charity, encouraged him to be kind to those who disagreed and to cease in disturbing the peace of the church on the issue of hymns.

Watts's life captures the monumental shift in English-speaking worship. He was born into a Non-Conformist or Congregationalist family, and his father was a leading deacon. He was the first of nine children and precocious from the start. He loved words and language. He began the study of Latin at the age of four, the study of Greek when he was nine, French at eleven, and Hebrew at thirteen.

He also loved to make words rhyme, even in everyday conversation. When he was caught with his eyes open during family prayers, he replied,

A little mouse for want of stairs

Ran up a rope to say its prayers.

This annoyed his father, who spanked him and warned him to stop rhyming. The young Isaac reportedly replied,

Oh, father, do some pity take,

And I will no more verses make.

When he was a teenager, Watts complained to his father about the boring and monotonous way the congregation sang what were sometimes awful psalm doggerel, such as:

Ye monsters of the bubbling deep,

Your Master's praises spout;

Up from the sands ye docclings peep,

And wag your tails about.

He said people sang with "dull indifference" and "a negligent and thoughtless air." His father shot back, "All right, young man, you give us something better."

And so, he did. That same night, the congregation sang a new hymn by Watts, and here is the first stanza:

Behold the glories of the Lamb

Amidst His Father's throne;

Prepare new honours for His Name

And songs before unknown.

During his lifetime he wrote about 750 hymns—"songs before unknown." Many hymnals are studded with Watts's hymns—"When I Survey the Wondrous Cross," "Jesus Shall Reign Where E'er the Sun," "Our God, Our Help in Ages Past," and more.

Watts was also a prodigious scholar who produced sixty tomes of theology and philosophy, including a widely used textbook in logic, entitled *Logic, or the Right Use of Reason in the Enquiry After Truth With a Variety of Rules to Guard Against Error in the Affairs of Religion and Human Life as well as in the Sciences.* Despite the long title, Watts's treatise was a required text at Oxford University and went through twenty editions.

There are two features of Watts's life that bear on his magnificent production of spiritual songs.

First, he never married. One woman, Elizabeth Singer, fell in love with his hymns. You might say she met him over the Internet, but when she met him she was shocked. He was, she said, "only five feet tall, with a sallow face, hooked nose, prominent cheek bones, small eyes, and deathlike color." She quickly refused his matrimonial proposal, saying, "I like the jewel, but not the setting." That was as close as Watts ever came to marrying someone. His heart was poured into his hymns.

Second, he was a sickly man. Though ordained as a Congregation-alist minister, his health failed early in his ministry. Fortunately, he was befriended by the Lord Mayor of London, Sir Thomas Abney, and his wife Lady Abney, with whom he stayed for thirty-six years until his death. When asked about the amazing duration of the stay of their distinguished guest, Lady Abney gave an eloquent description of hospitality: "It was the shortest visit a friend ever paid a friend." Watts's meager energy exploded into his prolific poetry. His unseen congregation became the world.

The tune nearly always used for "Joy to the World" is "Antioch," but like the text, it didn't start out that way. Scholars have discovered a complex lineage of tunes, usually "attributed" to Handel's "Messiah" and arranged by the American Lowell Mason in 1836. The authoritative *New Oxford Book of Carols* argues that the author was probably William Holbrook, who pub-lished it in his nineteenth-century hymnbook, *Voce di Melodia* (c. 1836). Even though Holbrook appealed to antiquity and authority by attributing the tune to Handel's masterpiece, *The New Oxford Book of Carols* says "any resemblance to Handel was probably coincidental, or at least, unconscious." William E. Studwell has declared Handel's connection to the carol "com-pletely bogus."

Whatever its origin, it is clear that the tune's decisive moment came through an arrangement by Lowell Mason in his hymnbook published in 1836. If Watts is the father of English hymnody, Lowell Mason (1792–1872) is the father of American church music. He wrote the tunes to more than 1,600 hymns, including two of Watts's most famous poems: "I Sing the Mighty Power of God" and "When I Survey the Wondrous Cross."

Mason was a musician with a passion for democracy. He introduced music to American public schools and is called the first significant music educator in the United States. He started his career as a banker, blending the worlds of money and melody, but his heart was always in music and especially church music. He served for many years as the music director of the Fifth Avenue Presbyterian Church in New York City. There he radically altered the worship life away from professional choirs, providing the music to congregational singing accompanied by organ music. Before coming to New York, he was choir director and organist at the Independent Presbyterian Church of Savannah, Georgia, and under his leadership that church created the first Sunday school for black children in America.

Mason is remembered chiefly for integrating into his hymn tunes the music of European classical composers and emphasizing congregational singing. The work of American composers largely fell by the wayside for a while, and yet the idea that congregations provide most of the music in worship prevailed in Protestantism until the arrival of contemporary Christian music performed by "worship teams" and "praise teams" and accompanied by guitars, drums, and other instruments.

A common theme runs through the story behind "Joy to the World." Isaac Watts, a sickly, reclusive man, wrote poetry that everyone could understand. In "Joy to the World" he extolled the magnificent power of God and issued the summons to "let every heart prepare Him room." Lowell Mason, the composer who brought church music to the masses, wrote melodies so that every man and woman and child could sing "the glories of His righteousness, and wonders of His love."

Christmas is for everyone. It is joy to the entire world.

MEDITATION

Do You Hear the Singing?

After singing this carol all my life, I suddenly noticed something I'd missed: throughout this carol all of heaven and earth are singing! Do you hear the song?

Notice what Isaac Watts urges us to hear: "Let *earth* receive her King" He could have written, "Let *us* receive our King," but he's calling all the earth to respond to the arrival of little Lord Jesus. Then he has us sing the refrain three times, "And *heaven* and *nature* sing." Then in the second verse we sing again, "While *fields* and *floods, rocks, hills,* and *plains* repeat the sounding joy."

How many of us have ever heard a rock singing, or a field, a hill, or a river? Julie Andrews sings, "The hills are alive with the sound of music," but we hardly ever hear a preacher exhorting us to listen for the music that, according to Watts, is all around us. Apparently, we've missed an entire chorus in the heavens and on the earth to which Scripture, and especially Jesus, urge us to be listening.

How did we ever get so bookish that, instead of listening to the voices of nature, we go looking for God's presence in books rather than in brooks? This is not to disregard the importance of that book of books, the Bible; however, even the Bible tells us to get outdoors to glimpse the glory and hear the harmony.

"When I look at your heavens, the work of your fingers, the moon and stars that you have established; what are human beings that you are mindful of them, mortals that you care for them?" sings the Psalmist (Ps. 8:3–4). Just one deep breath under the starry sky can remind us of how minor our major worldly worries are in contrast to the immense grandeur of creation. If you want to consider this with what modern astronomy has taught us, just look up at the heavens on any clear night and locate the constellation Orion (you don't need a telescope). The giant red star in the upper-left corner of that constellation is Betelgeuse. The light entering your eyes from that star has been travelling since the year 1375 at the speed of light (186,000 miles per second). That's how far away just this one star is from our tiny earth—and Betelgeuse is 890 times wider than our Sun! And you think you're big and important?

But if that's too much, just enjoy the everyday world as Jesus did. Evidently, he spent more time watching nature than reading Scripture. "Look at the birds," he says; they'll remind you that your heavenly Father will provide your daily bread, just as He feeds them. Then too, "Consider the lilies of the field," because their simple beauty will teach you that God will provide you with enough clothing—not the world's "enough," but the "less is more" rule of real beauty. Jesus evidently loved being in gardens so frequently that Judas knew where to find him on the night of his betrayal. "Now Judas, who betrayed him, also knew the place, because Jesus often met there with his disciples" (John 18:2).

Even Paul, who seems far more bookish and theological than Jesus, speaks a strong word for God's self-revelation in nature. Writing to the Romans (Rom 1:20), he says that we have no excuse for not knowing about the greatness of God because "ever since the creation of the world, his eternal power and divine nature, invisible though they are, have been understood and seen through the things he has made." Paul says it even more beautifully when he preaches to the Athenians, reminding them that the God who is "Lord of heaven and earth" (Acts 17:24) is not a prisoner of our shrines. "Indeed he is not far from each one of us. For in him we live and move and have our being" (Acts 17:27, 28).

"Say your prayers in a garden early, ignoring steadfastly the dew, the birds and flowers, and you will come away overwhelmed by its freshness and joy," wrote C. S. Lewis, who was very much a scholar immersed in his books. There's a music out there, but you can hear it only with spiritual ears. Still, get out there (or look out of your window if you can no longer walk well), and you'll hear "heaven and nature sing." Jesus still often meets there with his disciples.

Let All Mortal Flesh Keep Silence

Unison

1 Let all mor-tal flesh keep si - lence, and with fear and trem - bling stand; pon-der noth-ing earth - ly mind - ed, for with bless-ing in his hand Christ our God to earth de - scend - eth, our full hom-age to de - mand.

2 King of kings, yet born of Ma - ry, as of old on earth he stood, Lord of lords, in hu - man ves - ture, in the bod-y and the blood, he will give to all the faith - ful his own self for heaven - ly food.

3 Rank on rank the host of heav - en spreads its van-guard on the way, as the Light of light de - scend - eth from the realms of end - less day, that the powers of hell may van - ish as the dark-ness clears a - way.

4 At his feet the six - winged ser - aph, cher - u - bim, with sleep - less eye, veil their fac - es to the Pres - ence, as with cease-less voice they cry, "Al - le - lu - ia, al - le - lu - ia, al - le - lu - ia, Lord most high!"

Let All Mortal Flesh Keep Silence

This hymn was written a long time ago, probably in the fifth century. It comes from Eastern Orthodox Christianity, and it appeared as part of the Liturgy of St. James of Jerusalem. This St. James was one of the twelve apostles and became the first bishop of Jerusalem. He is distinct in the New Testament from James, son of Zebedee, and James ("the Just"), the brother of Jesus. Unfortunately for him, he is known as James the Less or Lesser, "the minor," "the little," or "the younger." His father was Alphaeus and his mother was Mary, perhaps a cousin of Mary, the mother of Jesus. Some scholars argue that he was the author of the letter of James.

As with many things in the Bible, experts disagree about all this. What is clear is that the Eastern churches developed differently and eventually separately from those of the Roman Catholic Church (the Western churches) and, of course, Protestantism. The Eastern churches were and still are distinct in church government, theology, and worship.

On Christmas Eve, the Eastern churches use the Liturgy of St. James to celebrate the Last Supper, and the text of "Let All Mortal Flesh Keep Silent" comes from "The Prayer of the Cherubic Hymn." This fifth-century composition was sung as the elements of Communion were brought into the church.

That was 1,600 years ago. Now fast-forward to the nineteenth century. The Reformation represented a decisive break with the Roman Catholic Church, which was already different from Eastern Orthodoxy. The cry of the Reformers was "Sola Scriptura!" That meant that if it wasn't in the Bible, it shouldn't be in the church. A fascinating Protestant view of church history emerged: Start with Jesus, jump to the Reformation, and then trace Protestant developments to the present day. It left out all of Eastern Orthodoxy, with its massive influence in the Mediterranean world, Africa, and Asia. It eliminated all of the early and medieval developments of western Christianity.

It reminds me of an old *Peanuts* cartoon. Linus is sitting at a table, pencil and paper in hand. Charlie Brown asks him, "What are you doing?"

Linus replies, "I'm writing the history of our church." Then Linus begins to scrawl, and his first sentence is: "Our pastor was born in 1930."

That parochialism could not endure forever, but it lasted a very long time. Beginning in the nineteenth century, especially in England, thoughtful pastors and scholars began reclaiming the richness of early and medieval western Christianity and Eastern Orthodoxy, including its worship. It was called the Oxford Movement, and it gained strength and an even broader focus in the twentieth and twenty-first centuries. Today, historians of Christianity agree: the history of the church is the story of world Christianity, including Africa, Asia, and Latin America.

The leaders of the Oxford Movement were skilled in Latin and Greek, and Gerard Moultrie (1829–1855) translated the text of "The Prayer of the Cherubic Hymn" from the Greek. His paraphrase was published in *Lyra Eucharistica* (1864). Some of the Oxford Movement figures became Roman Catholic, but Moultrie remained within the Church of England, serving as a priest and chaplain and writing and translating hymns from Latin, German, and Greek.

"Picardy," the awe-inspiring tune for this Christmas hymn, has a fascinating and inspiring story. It's the melody of a French folk song from the province of Picardy in northern France, probably arising in the seventeenth century. The folk ballad told the story of Lazarus and the rich man (Luke 16:19–31), which is part of a longer section in Luke where Jesus teaches his disciples about money.

The poor man Lazarus lay at the gate of the rich man. Lazarus was "full of sores" and "desired to be fed with what fell from the rich man's table; moreover, the dogs came and licked his sores." Lazarus "died and was carried by the angels to Abraham's bosom." The rich man also died, went to Hades, and when he witnessed Lazarus in the bosom of Abraham, he pleaded with Abraham to let Lazarus "dip the end of his finger in water and cool my tongue." Abraham replied, "Son, remember that you in your lifetime received your good things, and Lazarus in like manner evil things; but now he is comforted here, and you are in anguish. And besides all this, between us and you a great chasm has been fixed."

Out of Jesus' story of the "great chasm" between the rich and the poor came a religious song (one of only a few in the French folk tradition) and a haunting tune by Mademoiselle Pierre Dupont, who remembered it from her childhood in Picardy and published it in 1860. It was harmonized by the great English composer Ralph Vaughn Williams for the *English Hymnal* (1906).

The simplicity of the tune often means that it is sung by children, quite understandably but perhaps wrongly. The music for "Let All Mortal Flesh Keep Silence" is rooted in Jesus' prophetic teaching about wealth and how the poor shall inherit the earth. Hymnologist Archibald Jacob saw the bite in the music when he wrote: "There is no childlike mirth or gaiety here whether the tune be sung fast or slow. In the present instance it must be sung very slowly, when its character appears rather somber, but at the same time dignified and ceremonious." Jacob continued, "If, however, it is sung fast, the sombreness changes to fierceness, and though it may suggest a dance, it is a dance of no amenable kind." Jacob concluded, "All tunes change their character, to a certain degree, with a considerable change of speed, but the cleavage here is of a very remarkable nature, and denotes an unusual tune."

The chasm between the rich man and Lazarus, the cleavage in the music—these capture an often suppressed theme in the story of how God became human in Jesus Christ. In the midst of the romance of Christmas, we often overlook the sobering question posed in Malachi 3:2 and sung every Christmas in Handel's "Messiah": "But who may abide the day of his coming, and who shall stand when he appeareth? For he is like a refiner's fire."

MEDITATION

The Camp Is Closed

Oskar Schindler was a German businessman who saved the lives of more than a thousand mostly Polish-Jewish refugees during the Holocaust by employing them in his factories. The record of persons whose lives were saved by his actions came to be called Schindler's List. A movie by that name was made in 1993 to tell their story.

Several years ago, I attended a university lecture delivered by a man who was a survivor from Schindler's List. I can't recall all the details of his story: how he got on that list as a young boy, somehow remained on that list despite many occasions when he could have been sent off to the gas chambers, how he was liberated with the arrival of the American troops, after that cared for by a gang of Hungarian bandits, and finally taken to England where he received a university education that prepared him for his career.

The part of his story I shall never forget is of the day of his liberation. On that morning, he woke up to discover that everyone was gone. No one had awakened him for another day of grinding toil. The other prisoners who worked beside him had disappeared, and the German guards were nowhere to be seen. In a kind of daze, he wandered out into the prison yard, expecting as always to see guards at the gate. Instead, the gates were open and other soldiers were there—but the soldiers were not wearing German uniforms.

One of the soldiers beckoned to him in a friendly manner. Knowing nothing other than to obey any guard's order, he walked hesitantly toward the soldier, an American, who held out a friendly hand to him, a hand holding a candy bar. After he had hastily devoured the candy bar, what else was there to do but wander off? Everyone was gone. There was nowhere else to go but away—the camp was closed! And even if one did not know where to go next, why would anyone want to stay around that place of death?

What I hear in the words of this ancient hymn is a story of liberation. From heaven's realms of endless day, the Light of Lights descends to earth, flooding our world with light so "that the powers of hell may vanish." Can it be true that such a day of light has actually dawned? Has the hellish camp really been closed?

Whenever we sing this hymn at Christmas, my mind goes to another hymn that we sing at Easter (and sometimes at memorial services for loved ones). I don't know why, but I've never heard an Easter sermon that announces the momentous victory that this hymn proclaims: "He closed the yawning gates of hell; the bars from heaven's high portals fell."

Have you ever heard a preacher declare that hell is closed and that there's no place else to go but heaven? Many of us have sung those words through a lifetime of Easters, but somehow never noticed what we were singing; it seems all too good to be true. But the closing words of our Bible speak of the heavenly Jerusalem as that city whose "gates will never be shut by day—and there will be no night there" (Rev 21:25). It sounds like our carol in which the Light of Light has descended, flooding our world with endless day, so that "the powers of hell may vanish."

The morning headlines never announce such unbelievably good news. The powers of hell seem as alive and well as ever. There's no need to itemize all the reasons for believing that the death camp of hell is still open for business and that all sorts of bad guys (unmistakably identified by those of us who are the good guys) will surely become inhabitants of that dark realm. It would be naïve to deny the awful conditions that exist in our world; however, the traditional picture of an unending battle between heaven and hell fails to tell the whole story. The real story is that heaven is endlessly open, although some people are still standing outside in the darkness. They haven't heard that the war is over and that there's no going back to the death camp.

On January 16, 2014, a famous Japanese soldier died. Hiroo Onoda was an intelligence officer of the Imperial Japanese Army during World War II. He did not get the news that the war had ended in 1945, but remained in the jungles of Lubang Island in the Philippines for almost thirty years until his former commander was sent from Japan to find him and personally convey official orders relieving him of duty. During his years in hiding, leaflets had been dropped from the air to inform any remaining soldiers that the war had ended, but Onoda thought that the leaflets were enemy propaganda.

I have been accused of spreading such enemy propaganda when I have proclaimed that the yawning gates of hell have been closed. Many people refuse that message and continue to live in the darkness outside the open doors of God's kingdom of love and grace. In that outer darkness, it's still a kill-or-be-killed, saved-or-lost world, a world in which the victory of God's love is not conclusive.

Will they remain out there forever? Can anyone resist the offer of God's forgiving grace forever? No one knows the answer to that ponderous question. But we do know that the gates will never be closed and that God never gives up on anyone. As in that parable of the Two Sons (Luke 15:11–32), when the elder son refused to come in to the banquet, the father remained with him in the outer darkness. The God of grace whose fatherly love was revealed in the life, death, and resurrection of Jesus Christ leaves no one behind! Even before Jesus, the Psalmist understood that merciful truth: "If I make my bed in hell (Sheol), you are there" (Ps 139:8)!

Lo, How a Rose E'er Blooming

1 Lo, how a Rose e'er bloom-ing from ten-der stem hath sprung,
2 I - sa - iah 'twas fore - told it, the Rose I have in mind;
3 This flower, whose fra-grance ten - der with sweet-ness fills the air,

of Jes-se's lin-eage com - ing as saints of old have sung.
with Mar - y we be - hold it, the vir-gin moth - er kind.
dis - pels with glo-rious splen-dor the dark-ness ev - ery-where.

It came, a flower-et bright, a - mid the cold of
To show God's love a - right she bore to us a
True man yet ver - y God, from sin and death he

win - ter, when half - spent was the night.
Sav - ior, when half - spent was the night.
saves us and light - ens ev - ery load.

Lo, How a Rose E'er Blooming

This carol has been called "one of the better carols of all time." Its soaring beauty and widespread popularity today obscures the often murky history of Christmas carols and how confessional differences produce various words.

The author of the words is unknown. It was probably composed in Germany during the late fifteenth or early sixteenth century as a Christmas or Twelfth Night folk carol. The earliest manuscript (1580) comes from St. Alban's Carthusian monastery in Trier in the Rhineland, and then it appeared in three books in 1582, 1599, and 1608. Each book had a different number of stanzas, ranging from six to twenty-three. "Lo, How a Rose "E'er Blooming" has been translated eleven times into English alone, not to speak of multiple versions in German and other languages. Today, it usually appears with three verses, but sometimes the third verse varies from hymnbook to hymnbook.

The carol draws on two passages from the Old Testament. The carol was probably part of the veneration of the Virgin Mary in late medieval Catholicism, and so the reference was the Song of Solomon 2:1: "I am a rose of Sharon, a lily of the valleys." The church taught that Mary was "the rose of Sharon" without thorns. Later, however, Protestants used Messianic imagery and interpreted the reference to "a rose" through the lens of Isaiah 11:1: "There shall come forth a shoot from the stump of Jesse, and a branch shall grow out of his roots." Jesus was the descendant of King David, the "shoot from the stump of Jesse," and therefore the "rose" of this carol.

Theodore Baker (1851–1934) translated the first two verses of this carol. A famous and very influential musicologist, Baker was literary editor of the music publisher, G. Shirmer, for thirty-six years, published the first major work on the music of Native Americans, and edited *Baker's Biographical Dictionary of Musicians*. The commonly used third verse comes from the translator Harriet Krauth Spaeth (1845–1925), but another verse translated by Gracia Grindal (1943–) is published in some hymnals.

Although the tune undoubtedly comes from the fifteenth century, it was given nearly lasting form by Michael Praetorius (1571–1621), one of the greatest musicians in church history, in his work, *Alte Catholische Geistliche Kirchengesänge* (1599), and in a harmonization published in 1609. Johannes Brahms composed a chorale prelude based on the tune of "Lo, How a Rose E'er Blooming" in 1896. Because of its somewhat difficult tune, it was more often sung by choirs, but in the late twentieth century, its appearance in hymnbooks soared. It is now a frequent part of congregational celebrations of Christmas.

Since the 1950s, it has also been widely performed by a wide variety of artists, such as Percy Faith, the Harry Simeone Chorale, the Robert Shaw Chorale, Linda Ronstadt, Charlotte Church, and Sting.

Anyone who has grown roses knows how difficult it is and how fragile the blossoms are. They can radiate beauty and symbolize love, but they grow amidst thorns and represent pain. The young girl Mary embodied that paradox—the beauty of a divine child born in human pain.

In the midst of our suffering, this carol reminds us of God's presence and deliverance; Jesus Christ is the ever-blooming rose.

MEDITATION

The Fragrance of Faith

"Isaiah 'twas foretold it, the rose I have in mind." No, 'twas not Isaiah! The passage cited as a basis for this carol (Isa 11:1) makes no mention of a rose. Instead, we see a shoot or twig emerging from the stump or trunk of a tree—but you and I have never seen roses growing out of the stumps or trunks of trees. All kinds of notions have "grown out of" this passage. The Hebrew word for "branch" (*netser*) could have been the source of Matthew's claim that Jesus would be called a Nazarean. Or the Latin Vulgate's rendering of "shoot" as *virga* prompted later commentators to connect the verse with the Virgin Birth. Wild, isn't it, how far imagination can take a biblical text?

But it really isn't wild; instead, it's standard procedure in the history of biblical interpretation. Technically, it's called *midrash*, and refers to the ancient practice of letting the Spirit of God work on the reader's imagination, allowing a multitude of possible interpretations emerge from the text.

Jesus himself engaged in such freedom in quoting from Hebrew Scripture, taking liberties in the selection or deletion of certain verses to establish his point of view.

In fact, something like this kind of imaginative interpretation seems to surround this carol that comes to us, probably, from the fifteenth century. In Roman Catholic understandings of this carol, the rose referred to the Virgin Mary. In later Protestant interpretations, however, the rose became Jesus. But what's the problem with either reading? There must have been something of roselike beauty about Mary, the mother of our Lord. And would not the fragrance of Mary's faith have been the atmosphere in which Jesus was nurtured, making his life sweet-scented in spiritual splendor? After all, shouldn't our lives be made fragrant by our faith? When we enter a room, shouldn't there be a lovely aroma that we carry with us because of our faith in Jesus?

Sadly, not all of us who profess to follow Jesus lead lives of aromatic attraction. Some of us are so "right" that no one wants to be around us. When I first became a Christian, there were so many "don'ts" about the lives of people in the church I attended that some of us were ugly with negativity. We didn't dance, smoke, drink, play cards, attend movies, or wear lipstick (girls only). It's true that smoking gives one stinky breath, but our "Miss Manners" moral certainty smelled so strongly of pride that it wasn't fun being around the self-righteous prudes we had become.

It's the same with the so-called "liberal" Christians. Like St. Francis, it is beautiful to live with reverence for the earth, but I have friends who go about environmental crusades with such an angry, all-knowing attitude that their lives are a denial of the entire Franciscan way of a peaceful and simple life. Indeed, their lives of personal indulgence, consumption, and "birdbath Franciscanism" are often obscene denials of genuine care for God's earth.

It's all a matter of growing in the beauty of humility. In contrast to angry liberals, there are so-called conservative Christians who read the wrong newspapers, watch the wrong TV channels, have all the wrong beliefs about gay people, war, and the environment, but speak so softly and live with such a liberality of kindness that you wonder if they're really as conservative as they profess to be. People often behave better than what their beliefs lead you to expect. When you're down and in need of forgiveness, there are certain tough-love conservative businessmen who will reach out to you with more grace and mercy than you'll receive from a liberal, biblically so-phisticated pastor.

The bottom line is that people are always better than their beliefs, and I think the secret difference is that some people, without even knowing it, or being able to articulate it, have somehow come close enough to the living Jesus to be seized by the spell of his compassion for the world, near enough to catch the fragrance of his lovely life. Whatever their belief system may be, they always come off as "smellin' like a rose."

Why are some Protestants such a disgrace to real reformation of life that they make me ashamed to be a Protestant? And why are some of my Roman Catholic friends so attractive in their devotion to both Mary and Jesus that they almost persuade me to convert? And why do so many non-Christians live and behave more in a Christlike manner than many Christians?

The only answer to these mysteries for me is that Jesus is still alive and well, walking about our world, still seeking friends who, even if they don't confess the correct creeds, will receive his spiritual presence and do his loving work in the world. Their lives are fragrant with Jesus' roselike beauty. Their lives are truly "mighty lak a rose."

Mary Had a Baby

Moderately Slow *(with tenderness)*

Ma - ry had a ba - by, Yes, Lord! Ma - ry had a ba - by,
What did she name him? Yes, Lord! What did she name him?

Yes, my Lord; Ma - ry had a ba - by, Yes, Lord! De
Yes, my Lord; What did she name him? Yes, Lord! De

peo-ple keep - a com - in' an' de train done gone.
peo-ple keep - a com - in' an' de train done gone. She

Mary Had a Baby

"Mary Had a Baby" is like most African American spirituals in that we know very little about its origins with any certainty. It may date to the eighteenth century and the island of St. Helena, part of the Sea Islands off the coast of Beaufort, South Carolina. This area is renowned because it might have been the site of the first introduction of slavery in what would become the United States, in 1526, long before the more commonly accepted date of 1619 in the Jamestown colony of Virginia.

The Sea Islands are also extremely important because the slaves there produced the Gullah language and culture. Since the Sea Islands were quite isolated from the mainland, the slaves developed a fascinating blend of linguistic and cultural elements of African and European life. Gullah is perhaps the most obvious and powerful example of how African traditions survived during and even after the forced migration of Africans to North America.

"Mary Had a Baby" is one of several African-American spirituals that honor Mary as the mother of Jesus. This theme is probably a product of the separation of fathers and mothers during slavery and the rise of matriarchal families, where strong women shaped the lives of their children.

"Mary Had a Baby" is also an excellent example of the call-response character of slave songs, undoubtedly drawn from the fields where one slave would sing a line and the others would respond. The call-response has left an indelible mark not only on the music but also the preaching and worship of African American churches to the present day.

In this carol, one verse is the call; the next is the response: "What did she name him?" "She named him King Jesus." Although most hymnbooks contain the five verses in our reprinted version, the carol originally had several more that were set in the call-response motif following the first verse ("Mary Had a Baby"). *The Second Penguin Book of Christmas Carols* (1970), edited by Elizabeth Poston, includes these verses:

> "Where did she lay him?" etc.
>
> "Laid him in a manger" etc.

"What did she name him?" etc.

"Name him King Jesus" etc.

"Who heard the singin'?" etc.

"Shepherds heard the singin'" etc.

The following verses depart from the call-response pattern and pick up the narrative:

"Star keep a-shining" etc.

"Moving in the elements" etc.

"Jesus went to Egypt" etc.

"Traveled on a donkey" etc.

"Angels went around him" etc.

In one carol, the slaves told virtually the entire story of the birth of Christ contained in Scripture.

Like so many other Christmas carols, "Mary Had a Baby" went through revisions, but one change is remarkable because it omitted a line that was sung at the end of every verse:

"The people keep a-comin' and the train done gone."

This line appears in the first publication of the carol in *St. Helena Island Spirituals* (1925), edited by N. G. J. Ballanta-Taylor, and in James Weldon Johnson and J. Rosamond Johnson's *The Books of American Negro Spirituals* (1925, 1926). In the relatively few contemporary hymnbooks in which "Mary Had a Baby" appears, "the people keep-a comin' and the train done gone" is often removed, perhaps because its meaning is unclear and seemingly irrelevant to the other lines of each verse.

Elizabeth Poston suggested that "the imaginative impact upon the mind of the Negro of the advent of the railroad, 1830–1840, is reflected in the sort of refrain in true ballad tradition, in which there is nothing incongruous in a refrain not necessarily related to the matter of the song." This explanation might shed light on other ballads but probably not on "Mary Had a Baby." The slaves of the South Sea Islands scarcely ever witnessed a train because of their geographical separation from the mainland. What they knew about trains undoubtedly came from their white owners and overseers.

Here again is the double meaning of African American spirituals, as well as the apocalyptic theme of God's righteous judgment against human injustice.

Who are the people coming for the train? White people.

What is the train? It's bound for heaven—freedom, salvation, and union with God.

What happens when white people come to the station? The train "done gone."

When we sing "Mary Had a Baby," we declare the joyous birth of our Savior. It's a sweet, slow, and perhaps even saccharine celebration of the arrival of the Messiah. But that divine advent comes with a warning, for the slaves knew the will of the Lord:

"Let justice run down like water,

And righteousness like a mighty stream" (Amos 5:24).

This Christmas, as we ponder that brave, young mother and the "King Jesus" in her arms, we might ask ourselves: What train are we missing?

MEDITATION

O Mary!

"O Mary, conceived without sin, pray for us who have recourse to thee."

Those were the words imprinted on the tiny gold Miraculous Medal that the nurses at St. Joseph hospital pinned to the baby blanket on the day I was taken home following my birth in 1928. I have often wondered what those holy sisters were thinking or hoping as this newborn child of a Protestant mother left the hospital that day. Some of their hopes may have been realized as my mother kept that medal pinned to my undershirt for many years thereafter.

I never asked what it meant; it was attached there for many years, accompanied during the winter months by a tiny cloth bag of camphor to ward off chest colds. Did my mother hope to ward off other evil spirits by this medal, or was it there just in case the Catholics were right? I never asked, nor can I remember ever asking to have it removed.

What I do remember is that, during my junior high school years, an adult version of the medal came in the mail. This one had a silver chain so that it could be worn about the neck, and I actually began wearing it. Had my mother remained in some kind of contact with whatever society sent that medal? Again, I never asked. What I do remember is the part that it played in my life during the summer of 1942.

I spent most of that summer in Rochester, New York, as my mother took care of an ailing aunt. It must have been a lonely summer for me without my regular playmates. Almost every day I walked alone to the Seneca Park Zoo where I rode the old merry-go-round until I could no longer catch the brass ring for a free ride. The really odd routine was my daily walk to a vacant lot where I would repeat the prayer on the Miraculous Medal.

What was I thinking of? Was this what the nuns were hoping for when they pinned it on my blanket fourteen years earlier? Or was it that I just felt some need to do something religious? I can't remember ever talking to Mary, as some Christians "have a little talk with Jesus" during the course of their day; I simply repeated the words of the prayer, with neither any notion of what they meant, nor with any remote idea of the meaning of the doctrine of the immaculate conception.

Were these somewhat bizarre prayers of a lonely kid being heard somewhere? Or was it as Dorothy Day once wrote about the outcome of her early dedication to Virgin Mary, "all the little contacts with her that brought me to Him"? Someone must have been listening because, three years later, other circumstances brought me to him and, eventually, into the ministry of the Presbyterian Church.

Many years later at the University of Detroit, in a post-graduate class, all the members of which were either Jesuit priests or Sisters of Mercy, the professor suggested on the first day that we get to know one another by sharing what we remember of our first prayers. When I recited the prayer on my medal, my fellow students must have thought that I was either a lapsed Catholic, or else that this was the dawn's first light of an unimaginable rapprochement with Protestantism.

While it may shock Protestant readers, I want to state that we can't get nearer to Jesus than Mary. Of course, I don't say that in the sense in which my devout Catholic friends believe it true. I say it more as one who has read much of the scholarly literature about the search for the historical Jesus. In that sense, no one could tell us more about Jesus than Mary, if only we could ask her. If I were to answer the question, "With whom, of all the notable figures of history would you want to have lunch?" my answer would be Mary.

What fascinating questions I'd put to her: What was he like as a little boy? Was he a perfect child, or was he truly human like other kids?—after all, he got lost once when they were visiting Jerusalem. And what did you teach him about God? And how did you say prayers with him at bedtime?

I suspect that I know the probable answer to that last one; at least, I think that Scripture hints at what was Mary's most frequent prayer with him. When she first learned that she was to accept the terrible burden of becoming a pregnant, unmarried teenager, her response to God was, "let it be with me according to your word" (Luke 1:38). And is there not a clear echo of that prayer in one of Jesus' last prayers when he too was asked to accept an impossible burden, "Thy will be done" (Matt 26:42)—not to mention those words as the opening petition of the prayer he taught his disciples?

God always answers those who offer that prayer in sincerity of heart, even if offered by Buddhists, Hindus, or even by those seemingly lost, godless, despairing souls who, "deprived of daylight, worship in the night." If God can hear the crazy prayers of a lonely teenager, God can hear the unorthodox prayers of anyone who yearns to do God's will.

"Mary had a baby, My Lord!" The whole project was outrageous from the beginning. But isn't that like our God whose foolishness is wiser than human wisdom (1 Cor 1:25)? Hail, Mary!

O Come, All Ye Faithful (Adeste Fidelis)

1 O come, all ye faith - ful, joy - ful and tri - um - phant, O
2 Sing, choirs of an - gels, sing in ex - ul - ta - tion,
3 Yea, Lord, we greet thee, born this hap - py morn - ing,

come ye, O come ye to Beth - le - hem;
sing, all ye cit - i - zens of heaven a - bove;
Je - sus, to thee be all glo - ry given;

come and be - hold him, born the King of an - gels;
glo - ry to God, all glo - ry in the high - est;
Word of the Fa - ther, now in flesh ap - pear - ing;

Refrain

O come, let us a - dore him, O come, let us a - dore him,

O come, let us a - dore him, Christ, the Lord.

O Come, All Ye Faithful (Adeste Fideles)

A bsolutely ethereal and universally beloved—that's the unanimous ver-
dict on "O Come, All Ye Faithful." It is ecumenical, equally used by
both Roman Catholics and Protestants. It has been translated into more
than one hundred languages, and it has appeared in nearly 600 English-
language hymnbooks alone. Its phenomenal capacity to transcend both
Christian traditions and national boundaries makes it perhaps *the* carol of
every Christmas season.

Like so many carols, the origins of "O Come, All Ye Faithful" were
once unknown and contested. Because it first appeared in Latin, people
thought it must be old—perhaps an ancient piece sung and danced around
the crèche. Some attributed it to Saint Bonaventure (1221–1274), a follower
of St. Francis of Assisi; the Germans; the Cistercian order of monks; and/or
the seventeenth-century-English musician John Redding.

In fact, this carol is much more modern. Anything as popular as "O
Come, All Ye Faithful" was bound to attract the attention of historians. They
are the scholarly version of detectives, and eventually they often solve what
in this case was called a "tantalizing problem, much like a jigsaw puzzle."
The breakthrough came in 1947 from Dom John Stéphan, a Benedictine
monk. In the archives of the famous Roman Catholic center of theology and
scholarship in Douai, France, Dom Stéphan found a manuscript of "Adeste
Fideles" that is undoubtedly the work of John Francis Wade (1711–1786).

Like many who fled to Douai, Wade was an English Catholic. By
profession, he was a teacher of Latin and a "copyist," a kind of eighteenth-
century duplicating machine. With usually beautiful calligraphy, copyists,
who had a long and venerable tradition, would create multiple versions of
documents deemed unnecessary or unfeasible to print. Like editors, copyists had a derivative trade, living off other people's words, so it first appeared impossible to scholars that a copyist should have written a carol as
gorgeous as "Adeste Fideles." But Dom Stéphan found six texts of the carol,
all by Wade, and demonstrated that Wade not only wrote the Latin text but
was perhaps even the composer of the music—sometime between 1740 and

1743. The words were first published in France in 1760, and the Latin text was printed in England in 1782.

The English translation was rendered by Frederick Oakeley (1802–1880), an Anglican priest and member of the Oxford Movement, which sought to recover the richness of early and medieval Christianity. Because of his pre-Reformation affinities, Oakley was eventually forced out of the Church of England and became a Roman Catholic. He published an early translation of "Adeste Fideles" in 1841 and revised it several times to perfection. In 1852 it appeared in the form we sing it today. There are more than fifty other English translations, including the incredibly wooden version ("Hither, Ye Faithful, Haste with Songs of Triumph") that appeared in the American Presbyterian hymnal of 1843. Mercifully, Oakley's translation has prevailed throughout the English-speaking world.

The origin of the tune is still being debated. Some think Wade wrote it, but he may have borrowed it from a comic opera of the day written by Charles Simon Favart (or, others argue, Favart borrowed it from Wade). Some believe the tune was a popular melody drawn from Italy and Portugal and introduced to England through the Portuguese chapel in London. Hence, it is sometimes called "Portuguese Hymn" or, as the typically anti-Catholic American Presbyterian Lowell Mason called it during the nineteenth century, the "Romish Melody."

Its popularity is unquestioned. Dom Stéphan pointed out that at least one form of the tune is "one of the very few hymns that has found its place in every collection of Christian hymns." Equally stunning is the fact that no other tune has ever been associated with "O Come, All Ye Faithful." Historian Douglas Brice has concluded that "O Come, All Ye Faithful" is "the carol that more than any other has endeared itself to the hearts of Christians the world over. Without being a folk-song it is an international possession."

The carol is usually sung at the end of Christmas services of lessons and carols—with good reason. "O Come, All Ye Faithful" is a summons. It is a call to rise and witness to the Christ child, of whom "choirs of angels sing in exaltation" and "all ye citizens of heaven above" shall proclaim. It is a carol that should be sung not sitting down, but processing to the manger and then into the world. Across the centuries, its words beckon us to live, not for ourselves, but for God: "O come, let us adore him, Christ, the Lord."

MEDITATION

A Choir of Ordinary Citizens

It's not easy to get into a really great church choir. In any town, the church that has the best choir by professional music standards can choose who makes the cut to become a member of the choir. That's because money is a determining factor in what makes a really fine church choir. Ordinary folks who can hardly "carry a tune" just won't make it; for that matter, they won't even try to get into such a choir.

True, they may have enjoyed singing in the little choir back in their country church; they were good enough to belong to that small company of rural amateurs who gathered for choir rehearsal on Thursday night. Even old folks who had lost their voice continued to sing in that kind of choir. It was a happy group of ordinary folks who enjoyed just being together as much as they enjoyed trying to make music. Somebody always brought cookies or coffee cake, so they had refreshments after the rehearsal, and there was important sharing of joys and sorrows in that time of fellowship.

But it's not that way in the big city church choirs; no one has to tell ordinary singers that they don't belong in such a choir. Through most of my ministry I've been blessed by having such grand choirs. With a few exceptions, the organist/choir directors were fellows of the American Guild of Organists, some of whom played on the organ concert circuit. In one church, most of the members of the choir were paid professional singers, and in another church our soloists made it into opera or onto the Broadway stage. Lest all of this sound snobbishly professional, I must tell you that the really great ones possessed something more than what we call talent. You might call it a sense of calling, but it was even more than that.

The few really great singers had what I can only call a sense of citizenship. They had arrived at the realization that they were never playing or singing alone. They were always part of another choir that has a higher, heavenly allegiance. They did their singing and playing with "choirs of angels" and with "citizens of heaven above." They were somewhat like those early Christians who expressed their loyalty by saying "our citizenship is in heaven, and it is from there that we are expecting a Savior, the Lord Jesus Christ (Phil 3:20).

One of the finest choirmasters with whom I was ever privileged to work has gone on to sing with those choirs of angels and, in the lovely humility of his life down here on earth, would never want me to describe him as "great." He and his wife chose to live as those who belong to what George MacDonald called "the high country." Their decisions, their tastes, and their allegiances were guided by a sense of loyalty to a higher kingdom.

They lived very simply, raising their family in a little house on the other side of town, in the "lower-rent" district. They did not hobnob with the wealthy, even though their income would have allowed them to do so. Both of them were first-class performers on the two instruments in which they excelled. But more than that, when they raised their voices in song, some music from those highlands could be heard. Such a sense of higher citizenship, however, was costly and demanded personal sacrifice. In fact, it was this issue of a higher citizenship that cost Jesus his life.

We often fail to notice why Jesus was executed by the Roman Empire—and it was the Romans, and not the Jews, who decided to get rid of Jesus. It was Rome that was threatened by Jesus' message because his preaching was not like that of today's evangelists. Jesus didn't go about urging people to accept him as savior so they could go to heaven. Indeed, if that had been his gospel, Rome would have given his ministry financial support. What could have pleased Rome more than to have the common people of their vast empire focused upon a future heaven? With such a distraction, the multitudes would be happy with their earthly poverty, and Rome could have continued to exploit them without fear of uprisings.

But Jesus didn't talk about going to heaven. He talked about bringing heaven to earth, and urged us to pray daily for the coming of that other empire—"Thy empire come, Thy will be done." That's the real meaning of the Lord's Prayer. Jesus called people to transfer their allegiance to another empire, the empire of God, and that was traitorous, subversive talk. But Jesus and his followers lived joyfully as though they were already in that other kingdom; indeed, they lived mirthfully because it was a singing kingdom. It was as though they could already hear that "great multitude . . . from all tribes and peoples and languages, standing before the throne" (Rev 7:9). That great choir might someday even include their enemies, because they believed that even their Roman enemies could be "loved into" that singing kingdom as "citizens of heaven above."

My devoted organist's brother-in-law was a pastor of similar sympathies and a good friend of mine. He retired to a town in the mountains of Western Pennsylvania. What kept the town going was a factory of a multinational corporation, whose executives brought money and leadership into that church. Their wealth made it possible for what had been a little country church to have a paid organist and a fine choir. That lasted until the factory was closed, transferring the executives and their money elsewhere.

Just the little folks were left. They couldn't afford an organist, and the old lady who could play the piano didn't know how to play the organ. Without paid leadership, the choir fell apart. "So what we did," said my retired pastor and friend, "was just sing hymns. Our morning service became a hymn-sing with a brief sermon. But it was more heavenly than ever!"

Maybe the music of heaven won't be at all like that of our finest choirs on earth. Maybe it will just be the singing of the ordinary citizens of heaven.

O Come, O Come, Emmanuel

Unison

1 O come, O come, Em - man - u - el, and ran - som cap - tive
2 O come, thou Day - spring, come and cheer our spir - its by thine
3 O come, thou Wis - dom from on high, and or - der all things,
4 O come, De - sire of na - tions, bind all peo - ples in one

Is - ra - el, that mourns in lone - ly ex - ile here, un -
ad - vent here; dis - perse the gloom - y clouds of night, and
far and nigh; to us the path of knowl - edge show, and
heart and mind; bid en - vy, strife and quar - rels cease; fill

Refrain (Harmony)

til the Son of God ap - pear.
death's dark shad - ows put to flight. Re - joice! Re - joice! Em -
cause us in her ways to go.
the whole world with heav - en's peace.

man - u - el shall come to thee, O Is - ra - el!

O Come, O Come, Emmanuel

The setting is a monastery in the ninth century. It's the Advent week before Christmas—the seven days before Christmas Eve. It is late afternoon or early evening, and the monks are gathered for the vesper service of prayer. They sing a Latin chant or plainsong—a single line of unaccompanied music—based on the "Kyrie" ("Lord, have mercy upon us"). This particular week they are singing the "O Antiphons," a call-and-response form of the plainsong. One part of the choir sings to the other, or one of the leaders of the monastery sings to the choir, and then the choir responds—back and forth. The "O" corresponds to the "O Come" that we sing today in "O Come, O Come, Emmanuel."

Each day they sing a different antiphon, using the seven titles of the Messiah: O Wisdom, O Lord of Might, O Root of Jesse, O Key of David, O Dayspring, O Desire of Nations, O Emmanuel—all drawn from the Old Testament. As *The New Oxford Book of Carols* points out, the titles form an acrostic—"Sarcore"—except in this case, the meaning became clear only when it was spelled backwards. It was actually "ero cras," meaning "I shall [be with you] tomorrow."

Worship in a monastery was complicated.

If this monastic song was the source of "O Come, O Come, Emmanuel," it would make it one of the oldest Christmas carols. Alas, the carol is probably more recent. The "O Antiphons" probably became *the idea* for the carol, but not *its origin*.

A Latin text of the "O Antiphons" was published in 1710 and was translated in 1851 by the venerable John Mason Neale (1818–1866) to create the earliest English version of the carol. A giant in the history of Christian music, Neale (pp. 46–47) gave English-speaking Protestantism some of its greatest hymns by mining the richness of early and medieval worship life. In 1853, Neale revised and improved the translation, and his frequent collaborator, Thomas Helmore (1811–1890), provided the haunting tune in their jointly published *Hymns Noted* (1854)—or "hymns with notes."

Where Helmore found his tune is disputed, but it is likely that it came from a fifteenth-century processional used by French nuns.

In short, as William Studwell has written, "What Neale and Helmore created was a medieval carol of nineteenth-century origin."

Another English version was published in 1906 by Thomas Alexander Lacey (1853–1931). In 1910, William Sloane Coffin (1877–1954), the long-time president of Union Theological Seminary in New York, translated and combined four verses into two.

Today, most hymnals print four verses, the first two by Neale and the last two by Coffin (which is what is reproduced here). One exception is the Presbyterian hymnal, *Glory to God* (2013), which contains all seven verses of Neale's translation.

Such a tangled history may be a barrier to experiencing the power of "O Come, O Come, Emmanuel." It is, after all, profoundly biblical, drawing on the prophet Isaiah in 7:3: "Behold, a virgin shall conceive and bear a son, and shall call his name Emmanuel," which was picked up in Matthew's gospel (1:23). Each of the seven verses, and even the four verses we usually sing, are filled with references to the Old Testament.

But even more importantly, as Morgan Roberts points out below, the idea of Emmanuel (God with us) is the central Christian affirmation about Christ's birth.

This prompts a story, drawn from my own life. For nearly all of my ministry, I have been a teacher, trying to educate people (and especially ministers-to-be) about the richness of the Christian witness throughout history. I became a seminary president and preached and lectured widely about what Christians believed in the past and what their faith could mean today. I published several books and articles.

Then, in my fifties, I crashed. I was emotionally, physically, spiritually spent. Despite a loving family and many friends, I felt completely alone. This utter isolation from God, from others, and from myself imprisoned me in anguish and depression. Finally, I offered a simple prayer several times a day: "God, open me up."

One morning I was slathering peanut butter on an English muffin, a very mundane setting for what happened. Suddenly, I felt a white light around me. It was bright but not blinding. It was warm and embraced me. I stood still and the light gradually subsided. As it disappeared, I heard a voice: "You are not alone."

That was the beginning of a new life for me. After teaching about the Jesus of history, I found Jesus newly alive in my own life, or rather, Jesus found me. The truth of Christianity moved the longest distance in the world—the eighteen inches from my head to my heart. Later, I remembered the words of a wise teacher in my youth: "You are not saved by an idea."

That is what "O Come, O Come, Emmanuel" is all about.

"You are not alone." "God is with us." It's not an idea. It's real.

So, as you sing this elegant and simple tune, give thanks and praise in the carol's words:

> O come, thou Day-spring, come and cheer our spirits by thine advent here;
>
> Disperse the gloomy clouds of night, and death's dark shadows put to flight.
>
> Rejoice, Rejoice! Emmanuel shall come to thee, O Israel.

MEDITATION

Emmanuel

For the earliest Christians, all of whom were Jewish, "The Bible" was what Christians call the Old Testament. The New Testament did not yet exist, so when those early Jewish Christians searched their Scriptures with new eyes as followers of Jesus, certain texts "jumped off the page," captured their attention, seemed to validate their new experience.

One of those texts dated back to the early eighth century BCE, when the prophet Isaiah told Ahaz, king of Judah, that God would guarantee the continuation of the Davidic dynasty by having one of his wives give birth to a son to be named *Immanu El* (with us God). Isaiah was *not* predicting the much later birth of Jesus, but it is easy to see how early Christians read it as a "sounds-like" text, a promise about the birth of Jesus, through whom they had experienced God being with them.

It's easy to see how Jesus came to be thought of as our *Immanu El* (Emmanuel or Immanuel) in the minds of poets and hymn-writers. In varying ways and degrees, Christians think of Jesus as the one who has made God's presence real to us. We may not call him Emmanuel in our personal prayers but, at least once a year, we sing this Advent carol in which we relive the hope of ancient Israel for deliverance from captivity in Egypt. The only difference is that now we think of Jesus as the one who has delivered us from our own spiritual captivity. In the death and resurrection of Jesus, we have experienced exodus from spiritual bondage. What was national exodus for Israel has become spiritual exodus for us. Freed from slavery, we are now traveling toward the promised land with God's presence guiding us.

People deal with this sense of divine presence in different ways. Some followers of Jesus seem to think about God's presence all the time. Brother Lawrence (1614–1691), a lay brother in a Carmelite monastery in Paris, has left us with a classic devotional book in which he encourages us to practice a continual sense of the presence of God. Some of you either have or are attempting to do that very thing, to be continually aware of a holy presence in your life—to pray without ceasing.

For others, however, it's a "now-and-then" experience. In stressful or frightening moments, they send up a little cry for help: "O Jesus, please help me!" or "Dear Lord, just help me make it through this one!" A friend who played "cocktail piano" in a hotel lounge once told me that the most frequent request of salesmen away from home during the week was the ballad, "Help Me Make It Through the Night." Sadly, for some of us, God, Jesus, Lord, Emmanuel (or whatever we name we employ) is sort of an emergency chaplain.

But we can all begin to try Brother Lawrence's practice of God's continual presence by realizing that there is a wonderful Someone who is always with us. And we all need such a Someone. When we're angry and hurt, driving through traffic as we rehearse how we're going to tell *them* off, or put *them* in their place, wouldn't it be better to talk it through with Someone, asking how we can see things differently, visualizing a peaceful conversation with *them*, how we might make friends with *them*?

But let's forget about *them*, and think of all the times when we need Someone to guide and govern our lives, thoughts, and actions in our own wilderness wanderings as we journey toward the promised land. Most of our lives are spent in private moments in which, all through the day, we entertain thoughts and make decisions that, eventually, affect the world. No one can know when I engage secretly in impure, selfish, dishonest, or hateful thoughts, the outcome of which, unknown to others, is making me into a good or bad person; however, there is Someone who is aware of those secret moments.

Also, there is Someone who knows my best secret moments—what I *didn't* do today. Someone knows what I *didn't* think today when I could have filled my mind with less-than-honorable thoughts. Someone knows when I could have gotten away with a dishonest deal, but *didn't*. That presence I am calling Someone knows and appreciates the fact that I did my best to get through today as the best self I could be as a follower of Jesus. And everyone in the world can cultivate such a sense of the friendly, supporting presence of God.

My old friend, Howard, operated an old-fashioned hardware store in the city where I served my first little church. Another friend of mine was a customer who came in one day looking for a rare tool, no longer available except in expensive specialty stores. When he asked about this tool, Howard said he had that very tool somewhere in the attic. Howard returned with the tool and offered it for sale at a ridiculously low price. When the customer replied by saying that it was worth ten times that price, Howard responded, "That just wouldn't be fair. Look at this label. I bought it in 1929 for this low price and it would be dishonest to sell it for a high price."

There was a holy presence, a Someone who helped Howard be an honest, decent, and true follower of Jesus, and made his life a blessing to others. We can all live with a continual sense of this Someone, this God with us, this Emmanuel, who has, indeed, come to ransom us from our captivity.

O Little Town of Bethlehem

1 O lit - tle town of Beth - le - hem, how still we see thee lie!
2 For Christ is born of Ma - ry, and gath - ered all a - bove,
3 How si - lent - ly, how si - lent - ly the won - drous gift is given!
4 O ho - ly Child of Beth - le - hem, de - scend to us, we pray;

A - bove thy deep and dream-less sleep the si - lent stars go by.
while mor - tals sleep, the an - gels keep their watch of won-dering love,
So God im - parts to hu - man hearts the bless - ings of his heaven.
cast out our sin, and en - ter in; be born in us to - day.

Yet in thy dark streets shin - eth the ev - er - last - ing Light;
O morn - ing stars, to - geth - er pro - claim the ho - ly birth,
No ear may hear his com - ing, but in this world of sin,
We hear the Christ-mas an - gels the great glad ti - dings tell;

the hopes and fears of all the years are met in thee to - night.
and prais - es sing to God the King, and peace to all on earth.
where meek souls will re - ceive him still the dear Christ en - ters in.
O come to us, a - bide with us, our Lord Em - man - u - el.

O Little Town of Bethlehem

It was Christmas Eve, 1865. The American preacher Phillips Brooks (1835–1893) was riding on horseback from Jerusalem to Bethlehem. He paused on what is known as "the Field of Shepherds" where the angels announced the birth of Jesus, and he gazed at the town ahead. Continuing on, he attended the service at the Church of the Nativity in Bethlehem on what is supposed to be the site of Jesus' birth. He was deeply moved and the experience was indelibly imprinted in his memory.

"I remember especially on Christmas Eve," he later wrote, "when I was standing in the old church in Bethlehem, close to the spot where Jesus was born, when the whole church was ringing hour after hour with the splendid hymns of praise to God, how again and again it seemed as if I could hear voices that I knew well, telling each other of the 'Wonderful Night' of the Saviour's birth."

Back at home in Philadelphia, Brooks pondered his trip to Bethlehem in his heart, and several weeks before Christmas in 1868, he penned the words to "O Little Town of Bethlehem." Although Brooks never married, he loved children. He told his organist, Lewis H. Redner (1831–1908), that he needed a tune the children of the Sunday school could sing. Redner agonized about the music up to the deadline. On Christmas morning he awoke with the tune in his head, fully harmonized. Two days later, six adults and thirty-six children sang "O Little Town of Bethlehem" for the first time. Brooks named the tune after his organist, "Lewis," but changed the spelling to spare him embarrassment: "St. Louis."

Brooks was literally a giant of a man. He was six feet, six inches tall and weighed 300 pounds. An Episcopal priest, he is frequently cited as the greatest preacher America has ever produced. He was educated at Harvard, taught Latin and Greek briefly and apparently badly, and then entered the Episcopal Theological Seminary in Virginia. After his graduation, he became the rector of major Episcopal churches in Philadelphia and Boston. Throughout his ministry he rejected offers of professorships, the post of preacher at Harvard, and the assistant bishopric of Pennsylvania. In 1891 he accepted the position of Episcopal bishop of Massachusetts but died only two years into his term.

As a preacher, his height made him a commanding presence. So did his delivery, for he was able to speak at the rate of 213 words a minute. His book, *Lectures on Preaching*, was based on a series of presentations at Yale in 1877 and is still in print. The first volume of his collected sermons (1878) sold more than 200,000 copies. Many of his sermons are considered classics. His reputation in the pulpit extended to England; in 1887 Oxford University awarded him an honorary Doctor of Divinity degree. He loved hymns and in his youth memorized more than 200.

Redner's tune, "St. Louis," is the one that is usually sung in the United States, although sometimes hymnals include the tune "Forest Green" by the giant of twentieth-century English music, Ralph Vaughn Williams (1878–1952). "Forest Green" is the only music used for "O Little Town of Bethlehem" in Great Britain, and Williams composed it based on the ballad "The Plough-Boy's Dream," which he obtained from a farmer in Surrey, England.

Few would question Phillip Brooks's profound and moving insights into the Christmas story and the human condition. Richard Watson in *The English Hymn* has written, "Brooks skillfully brings the reader from the contemplation of the scene itself to an awareness of its meaning for the individual believer. The transition is managed with consummate skill . . . . Brooks knows that 'Misery cries out to Thee,' and his Christmas hymn is a hope that the situation will change, that through the coming of Christ and the spread of Christian values, society will become better."

Watson concluded, "That hope must be the aim of all people of good-will." Indeed, Brooks wrote a carol for children that has become a prayer of every human heart—not only for his era but also for the ages to come:

The hopes and fears of all the years
Are met in Thee tonight.

MEDITATION

The Hopes and Fears of Little Kids

It wasn't necessary to attend Sunday school or church to learn Christmas carols during my childhood. We could become acquainted with them in public school. Nowadays that is not the case, but in any December during the 1930s, the weekly assembly included the singing of familiar carols. Just how this was accepted by the parents of my Jewish friend and classmate, Bobby Zuckerman, I do not know. Thankfully, we are no longer insensitive to the religious preferences of others and have made public schools religiously neutral.

Looking back on those times, I wonder how my classmates might have understood the words, "The hopes and fears of all the years are met in Thee tonight." If I had any hope at all during December, it would have been that I might find an electric train set under the Christmas tree at my grandmother's house. My gifts would be there because we had only a tiny artificial tree at our house. Alas, however, no such gift ever appeared. Cousin Ralph had a large, elegant train set. Because his parents had died, Ralph lived with my grandmother and aunts, so the reasoning of my parents may have been that one train set would suffice for the entire family—and I guess it did, because I can never remember feeling any great sense of loss on a train-less Christmas morning. After all, I had real trains running "in my heart."

We lived in a tiny house on the other side of town in a blue collar neighborhood called Bellevue. Even if it wasn't a classy place to live, Bellevue did have a truly beautiful view of the Mohawk Valley when one looked down from the top of our hill. Down there were woods in which I was allowed freedom to wander, and a stream for fishing and trapping muskrat (a source of good income for me in my teens).

Best of all, along the hillside leading to the valley were the main tracks of the Delaware and Hudson Railroad (the D and H, as we called it). I could hear those great steam locomotives at all hours of day and night. I knew when they were highballing into town on the downhill grade, and when they were chugging uphill, heading westward out of town. Better yet, in my ramblings in the valley, whenever I heard a train approaching, I could stand next to the tracks as close as possible and feel the sheer, ground-shaking power of those smoke-breathing behemoths. No dinky model train set could compare with those monstrous machines. And the lonely wail of their whistles at night—what dreams of travel and adventure they inspired in a little kid! What could be a better gift and more lasting treasure than that of having those great trains as an inward possession?

For that matter, what we possess inwardly is what can never be taken from us; treasures of the heart are ours forever. Graduation speeches often cite the statement (possibly made by Emerson) that, "What lies behind us and what lies before us are tiny matters compared to what lies within us." But what if our inward stuff is junk, accumulated over the years from poor parenting, outrageous fortune, or our own bad decisions?

In George MacDonald's *Sir Gibbie*, a lovely story of an orphan boy being raised in the highlands of Scotland by a poor but saintly lady, there is this memorable passage: "So, teaching him only that which she loved, not that which she had been taught, Janet read to Gibbie of Jesus, talked to him of Jesus, dreamed to him about Jesus; until at length—Gibbie did not think to watch, and knew nothing of the process by which it came about—his whole soul was full of the man, of his doings, of his words, of his thoughts, of his life. Jesus Christ was in him—he was possessed by Him. Almost before he knew, he was trying to fashion his life after that of his Master."

There is no Christmas gift we could ever give to our children compared to such an inward friendship with Jesus. Indeed, isn't such a gift what Christmas is all about? No, my hopes of finding an electric train under the Christmas tree were never realized; however, I was left with something far more lasting and wonderful. It would take me many years to appreciate this gift fully. If a kid can have trains running in his heart, he can also learn to have Jesus living in his heart.

Sometimes at night, now many years later, I hear the lonesome sound of a train whistling as it passes over a crossing on the tracks a few miles from our home. Then those magic years down in the valley come flowing back. As they do, I give thanks for loving parents who knew how to give me the best of gifts, the gifts of trust and freedom to roam and enjoy the gifts of that valley.

Most of all I am grateful for the eventual discovery that I was not alone in that valley, that there was One waiting to be discovered in the tiny house of my heart, One who is an everlasting, inward treasure, One who has been with me over the years through even the dark valleys, One who is living his risen life in me. My hope is that I'll always be possessed by him, fashioning my life after that of my Master.

Once in Royal David's City

1 Once in roy - al Da - vid's cit - y stood a low - ly cat - tle
2 He came down to earth from heav - en who is God and Lord of
3 Je - sus is our child - hood's pat - tern, day by day like us he
4 And our eyes at last shall see him, through his own re - deem - ing

shed, where a moth - er laid her ba - by in a
all, and his shel - ter was a sta - ble, and his
grew; he was lit - tle, weak, and help - less, tears and
love; for that child, so dear and gen - tle, is our

man - ger for his bed: Ma - ry was that moth - er
cra - dle was a stall: with the poor and meek and
smiles like us he knew: and he feels for all our
Lord in heaven a - bove: and he leads his chil - dren

mild, Je - sus Christ her lit - tle child.
low - ly lived on earth, our Sav - ior ho - ly.
sad - ness, and he shares in all our glad - ness.
on to the place where he has gone.

122

Once in Royal David's City

Imagine a group of unruly, young children. They wrestle. They compete over each other's toys. They taunt and tease. They care nothing for order, much less the Christian faith.

This was the audience for Miss Cecil Frances Humphrey (1818–1895). In 1848, she published *Hymns for Little Children*, which ambitiously set out to teach children the doctrines of the Christian faith. Fourteen of the hymns were drawn from the Apostles' Creed. "Once in Royal David's City" explained the phrase, "I believe in Jesus Christ . . . who was born of the Virgin Mary." The first line of the Creed, "I believe in God the Father Almighty, Maker of Heaven and Earth," became the basis for the widely popular hymn "All Things Bright and Beautiful," and "He was crucified, dead, and buried" inspired "There Is a Green Hill Far Away."

Her children's hymnbook became a huge hit and went through more than one hundred printings in the next fifty years. During her lifetime, she wrote more than 400 hymns, and one English commentator maintains that "no one has surpassed her as a writer for children."

The author of "Once in Royal David's City" is always listed as Cecil Frances Alexander, her married name. She composed the poems of her children's hymnbook before she married the Anglican priest William Alexander in 1848—the same year of the hymnbook's publication—and after their marriage she continued her hymn-writing for children as Alexander, rather than Humphreys.

She was born to wealth and privilege in Ireland. Her father was the Earl of Wicklow, and she grew up amidst "grand houses and the almost feudal society of southern Ireland." Some point to her elite status as the reason for some passages in her hymns, especially in "All Things Bright and Beautiful," and many of her poems reflect the strictures of Victorian morality. Like her contemporaries, she adored and idealized children—a sentiment that was probably a response to high infant mortality in nineteenth-century Britain.

As the wife of a prominent Anglican cleric, who eventually became Archbishop of Armagh and Primate of all Ireland, she devoted her life to the poor and disadvantaged. The profits from *Hymns for Little Children* were donated to an institute for the deaf that she founded with her sister. Each day she traveled miles to deliver food, warm clothes, and medical supplies to the impoverished people of nineteenth-century Ireland. Her husband wrote about her, "From one poor home to another she went. Christ was ever with her, and all felt her Godly influence."

A year after its publication in verse, "Once in Royal David's City" was set to music by Henry John Gauntlett (1805–1876), a lawyer, a famous organist, and the prolific composer of more than 10,000 hymn tunes. He was a child prodigy. At the age of ten he became the organist of the church where his father was an Anglican vicar. At the age of only thirty-seven, he was honored with the degree of Doctor of Music by the Archbishop of Canterbury, the first recipient in more than 200 years. The name of the tune, "Irby," is a puzzle because Gauntlett had apparently no connection with any of the three English towns of Irby.

"Away in a Manger" portrays Jesus as divine from the moment of his birth: "the little Lord Jesus laid down his sweet head" and "no crying he makes." In "Once in Royal David's City," Cecil Frances Humphrey Alexander gives us a different Jesus. For a woman who spent her life living among the rich but devoted to the poor, Jesus' life began in poverty and destitution:

> And his shelter was a stable, and his cradle was a stall:
> With the poor and meek and lowly, lived on earth, our Savior holy.

And her conclusion—for children and for us—is clear:

> Jesus is our childhood's pattern, day by day like us he grew;
> He was little, weak and helpless, tears and smiles like us he knew;
> And he feels for all our sadness, and he shares in all our gladness.

At the beginning of "Once in Royal David's City," the editors of *The English Hymnal* (1906, 1933) noted: "Suitable also for Adults."

Indeed.

MEDITATION

The Little Judge

It is almost impossible to consider this carol without hearing in the back of one's mind the majesty with which it is rendered at the beginning of the broadcast of the yearly service of Nine Lessons and Carols from King's College, Cambridge. From the opening verse, sung softly a cappella by a boy soprano, to the full organ crescendo on the final verse, reverberating into the heights of that inspiring sanctuary, there is no other hymn that captures so musically and magnificently the last judgment scene of Matthew 25:31–46. However, the words of the final verse offer an assurance of pardon that we might not notice in Matthew's imagery.

When we sing,

> And our eyes at last shall see Him,
> Through His own redeeming love,
> For that Child so dear and gentle
> Is our Lord in heaven above;
> And He leads His children on
> To the place where He is gone.

Just imagine! The great judge before whom we shall finally stand is a little child, the child Jesus! Of course, had we paid closer attention to Matthew, we might have realized that his judgment scene is meant to convey that very humble imagery. The sheep of the kingdom turn out to be those who have recognized the presence of Jesus in those easily forgotten little people of our world who are hungry, thirsty, naked, outcast, sick, or in prison. And those who suffer most from such afflictions are, of course, the children of the world.

In the hungry nations of the world, it is the children who suffer the long-term effects of childhood malnutrition. In the refugee camps, it is the children, many of whom have lost their parents, who are the most damaged. Since our prison system works mostly against the poor, it is the children left behind who suffer the lifelong consequences of such deprivation of a parent.

Several years ago, in tutoring a class of second graders, the writing exercise for the afternoon was to compose a letter to someone far away. I soon discovered that my little guy was trying to write to his father. "Why are you writing to your father?" I asked, wondering why his father was far away. "Because he's in prison," he answered. His answer made it clear to me why he was having problems with his work, why he became easily more tired than the other children, why school was such a challenge. In the years since that afternoon, he has moved on and is doing much better. Still, I wonder how long he will carry the sadness and pain of those early years when his father was in prison.

It is such children, multitudes of such children, who will be standing with little judge Jesus on that final day when we are judged. It is such little people who will ask us why we did not notice them, why we did not feed them, why we did not have time for them, and why we remained silent when their nations were the victims of our national agendas. Still, I find hope for my forgiveness in the fact that I will finally stand before such a child and before such children. It is always the little people of history who have suffered most who are the most forgiving.

In those Roman catacombs where the early Christians buried their dead, one frequently sees the inscription of the Good Shepherd, surrounded by his sheep, carrying a lamb on his shoulders. But what is most amazing is that every so often one sees a merciful variation on that theme, as the Good Shepherd carries instead a little goat. Those persecuted insignificant little members of God's kingdom somehow found it in their hearts to hope that their Savior would have mercy on their enemies. For us today who believe that it is our right to retaliate when attacked by our enemies, it seems impossibly, ridiculously merciful that those early persecuted Christians could believe that God's mercy would be extended to those who had subjected them to savage cruelties, but what else might we expect from those who followed one who had taught them to love their enemies?

Our final hope rests in "that Child so dear and gentle" before whom we will stand at the last day. The God who took the risk of coming to us as a weak, vulnerable baby is the one whom we need never fear when "our eyes at last shall see him." I do not mean to say that this will be a soft, sentimental mercy. Quite the opposite, it will be a severe mercy, such as parents experience when they have disappointed a child but still receive the child's forgiveness. Perhaps there must be a bit of hell even in heaven, the hell of realizing that we disappointed the child Jesus and all of his little friends—but still have been forgiven. Even so, it will be mercy upon mercy upon mercy when, at last, we see him.

Rise Up, Shepherd, and Follow

Leave yo' flocks an' leave yo' lam's, Rise up Shepherd an' fol-ler, fol-ler,

Leave yo' sheep an' leave yo' rams, Rise up Shep-herd an' fol-ler, yes, fol-ler,

Fol - ler, fol - ler, rise up Shepherd an' fol-ler, fol-ler, Fol - ler de star of

Last Time — Slower and softer by degrees.

Beth-le - hem,— Rise up Shep-herd an' fol ler.— If you fol - ler.—

Rise Up, Shepherd

1 There's a star in the east on Christ-mas morn. Rise up, shep-herd, and
2 If   you take good heed to the an - gel's words, rise up, shep-herd, and

fol - low. It will lead to the place where the Christ was born.
fol - low. You'll for - get your flocks; you'll for - get your herds.

Refrain

Rise   up, shep-herd, and fol - low.   Fol - low, fol - low;

rise up, shep-herd, and fol - low.   Fol - low the star of

Beth - le - hem.   Rise   up, shep-herd, and fol - low.

Rise Up, Shepherd, and Follow

This is another African American spiritual—with two significant features.

First, it is an authentic piece of black slave music. "Rise Up, Shepherd, and Follow" was first published in 1867, two years after the Civil War, in *Slave Songs of the United States*. That collection was based on music heard from African American slaves in Georgia and South Carolina. Since it appeared so soon after the Civil War, it means that it undoubtedly was an antebellum slave song and not one created and eventually published in the post-war period or the twentieth century.

Second, more than any other Christmas slave song, "Rise Up, Shepherd, and Follow," demonstrates the famous "double meaning" of many of the spirituals. We have seen this in "Mary Had a Baby" (pp. 96–102), and the examples of how slaves transformed heavenly references into earthly meanings are many. "Swing Low, Sweet Chariot" has veiled references to the Underground Railroad. Crossing over Jordan meant escape to freedom in the North. The crumbling of the walls in "Joshua Fought the Battle of Jericho" inspired the belief that the fortress of slavery would come tumbling down.

The former slave and eloquent abolitionist Frederick Douglass recalled in his autobiography the impact of these songs on his soul:

> I did not, when a slave, understand the deep meanings of those rude, and apparently incoherent songs. . . . They told a tale which was then altogether beyond my feeble comprehension; they were tones, loud, long and deep, breathing the prayer and complaint of souls boiling over with the bitterest anguish. *Every tone was a testimony against slavery, and a prayer to God for deliverance from chains* [my emphasis]. The hearing of those wild notes always depressed my spirits, and filled my heart with ineffable sadness. The mere recurrence, even now, afflicts my spirit, and while I am writing these lines, my tears are falling. To those songs I trace my first glimmering conceptions of the dehumanizing character of slavery. I can never get rid of that conception. Those songs still follow me,

to deepen my hatred of slavery, and quicken my sympathies for my brethren in bonds.

In this book, we are reproducing two versions of "Rise Up, Shepherd, and Follow." One version is how the Christmas song appears in many hymnals today that are designed largely for use in white churches. Note the refrain:

Follow, follow; rise up, shepherd, and follow.
Follow the star of Bethlehem. Rise up, shepherd, and follow.

The other version contains the text as it originally appeared in 1867. It has a different refrain:

Leave yo' flocks an' leave yo' lam's,
Rise up Shepherd an' foller, foller,
Leave yo' sheep an' leave yo' rams,
Rise up Shepherd an' foller, yes, foller;
Foller, foller, rise up Shepherd an' foller, foller,
Foller de star of Bethlehem,
Rise up Shepherd an' foller.

It doesn't take an act of wild imagination to see how "leave yo' flocks an leave yo' lam's" might embody both an aspiration and a summons for a slave, far beyond the idea of shepherds "keeping watch over their flocks by night" (Luke 2:8).

The renowned African American literary critic Sterling Brown interviewed former slaves and their children. More than a half-century ago, he concluded: "Some scholars who have found parallels between the words of Negro and white spirituals would have us believe that when the Negro sang of freedom, he meant only what the whites meant, namely freedom from sin. . . . Ex-slaves, of course, inform us differently. The spirituals speak up strongly for freedom not only from sin (dear as that freedom was to the true believer) but from physical bondage."

Slavery simply has not disappeared from the modern world. Girls are seized and forced into slavery in Nigeria. Sexual slavery is found on every continent in the world, including in the United States. Though their conditions are somewhat improved, migrant workers in the United States labor on what sometimes become contemporary plantations. The reasons may be complex, but the United States has the highest rate of incarceration of any country in the world, and five times as many African Americans as whites are imprisoned. Whether black or white, the inmates often labor, making goods for the free population.

So, as you sing "Rise Up, Shepherd, and Follow," think about freedom—freedom from the bonds of your own life. But think too of those whose bodies and souls are literally bound in servitude. Hear the words of this song of slavery, for they are words of hope for liberation. Recall the words of Paul, "For freedom, Christ has set us free" (Gal 5:1). That's what the shepherds found in Bethlehem, and that's why the slaves sang.

MEDITATION

Forget Your Flocks!

It may be that no Anglo-American can possibly understand the inner meanings of African American spirituals, at least not in any depth. It is, thus, with hesitation that I set out to write about this *spiritual* carol. I describe it that way because there's a spiritual depth I can only attempt to plumb in this song that comes from the depths of human confinement. Slave owners thought, erroneously, that Christian faith might pacify and tame their slaves. Quite to the contrary, these people, torn from their homeland and chained in cruel captivity, found a freedom inconceivable to their white masters in the Bible's stories. That's why there's a double meaning in spirituals; there was often a coded message in them that their white masters couldn't decipher. In fact, this spiritual reveals something that I myself have overlooked in the story of Jesus' birth.

As with another carol, *The First Nowell*, this one fails to notice that the shepherds did not see a star; they did not "Follow the Star of Bethlehem." The star was the guiding light for the Magi—and there *weren't* three of them, and they *didn't* arrive at the manger as in our neighborhood nativity scenes. Somehow or other, we are all careless about some of the details when it comes to Christmas. You can check these facts for yourself by reading the stories in Matthew and Luke carefully.

But there's a big biblical detail that the African slaves noticed that white preachers have been missing all along. When you understand the huge significance of Jesus' birth, "You'll forget your flocks, you'll forget your herds." Did that really happen? Luke's story makes it sound that way: "So they went with haste," we read (Luke 2:16). Did you ever try moving an entire flock of sheep "with haste"? I've annually transported a few sheep to our church's Christmas event. If it is a challenge getting just a few sheep into a horse trailer (and it is), can you imagine moving an entire herd? Sounds to me as though the Christ event was so big that they actually left their flocks, as in this spiritual. I've never heard a white preacher mention this odd possibility.

But maybe there's no way we can follow Jesus without leaving something behind. Maybe that's why we've ignored the radical response of the first disciples (John 1:18–20), how Peter and Andrew "immediately they left their nets and followed him." And then how James and John, with the same sense of urgency "left their father Zebedee in the boat with the hired men, and followed him." Imagine that—leaving their poor old Dad to run the business by himself, and go running off with this itinerant preacher from Nazareth!

My oldest daughter resides in Lewiston, New York. It was one of the terminal points of the Underground Railroad. A bronze statue by the Niagara River depicts a slave family in a rowboat, ready to embark for the final short voyage across the river to freedom in Canada. Hidden in the homes of the good people of Lewiston, runaway slaves were rushed to the riverside under cover of night for this last step to freedom. When the time was right, they left all that was unnecessary behind and fled to their liberation. This spiritual comes from the heart of a people who knew just that—how to "rise up" with haste, "and follow."

There's stuff that we'll have to leave behind if we want the fantastic freedom of following Jesus. There are details in our lives that, if we consider them carefully, can be left unattended. Someone has said, "In the last hour of life, no one will ever regret not having stayed overtime at the office to clear up their desk." Gerry, one of my best-ever staff members, kept a sign in his creatively chaotic office: "A neat desk is the sign of a disorderly mind." Gerry was the living proof of that maxim; his desk was downright disorderly, but he was one of the most creative colleagues with whom I've ever enjoyed working.

And this is true, not only at the office, but more importantly at home. Some of the happiest and healthiest homes I've known have been a bit untidy. Really loving parents care more about having happy and healthy children than maintaining the kind of *House Beautiful* décor that looks, unfailingly, as though professional decorators have just finished their work. Scheduling our time as parents also needs to be done with an awareness of what really needs to be left behind; forgetting our flocks can involve leaving behind big bunches of busywork and social proprieties that can be left to others.

It's amazing how "black and unknown bards of long ago" (James Weldon Johnson) gave us these songs that can teach captive white folks how to be truly free. Only a black saint and scholar could state it as clearly as did Howard Thurman: "The ante-bellum Negro preacher was the greatest single factor in determining the spiritual destiny of the slave community. . . . His ministry was greatly restricted, . . . but he himself was blessed with one important insight: he was convinced that every human being was a child of God. This belief included the slave *as well as* the master. . . . Thus his one message springing full grown from the mind of God repeated in many ways a wide range of variations: 'You are not slaves, you are not niggers; you are God's children.'"

You, yes, you! You are not a slave to any flock, fad, or fashion of what the world defines as proper business as usual. You are a child of God. You can "forget your flocks, forget your herds. Rise up, shepherd, and follow."

Silent Night

1 Si - lent night! ho - ly night! All is calm, all is bright
2 Si - lent night! ho - ly night! Shep-herds quake at the sight,
3 Si - lent night! ho - ly night! Son of God, love's pure light,

'round yon vir - gin moth-er and child; ho - ly in-fant, so ten-der and
glo - ries stream from heav-en a - far, heaven-ly hosts sing al - le - lu-
ra - diant beams from thy ho - ly face, with the dawn of re - deem - ing

mild, sleep in heav-en-ly peace, sleep in heav-en-ly peace.
ia; Christ, the Sav - ior, is born! Christ, the Sav - ior, is born!
grace, Je - sus, Lord, at thy birth, Je - sus, Lord, at thy birth.

Silent Night

Everyone has a favorite Christmas carol, and for most it's "Silent Night." Ian Bradley termed it "the world's favourite carol."

This carol's rise to popularity mirrors the story of "Amazing Grace," at first barely acknowledged as a proper hymn and now the most widely recorded piece of sacred music in the world. Likewise, "Silent Night" almost didn't make it out of the Tyrolean Alps, but today it is sung around the world in more than 140 languages.

The story of "Silent Night" is marked by both fact and legend. What is known with certainty is that the words were composed by a young Catholic priest, Joseph Mohr, who was serving in the tiny, obscure village of Oberndorf, near Salzburg—then, as now, the scene of some of the greatest music ever written or performed. Mohr was the son of an unmarried woman and a vagabond Austrian soldier, who deserted both the mother and son. Mohr entered the Catholic priesthood, and because of ill health, he was soon assigned to Obendorf to minister in the purer, milder air.

Mohr wrote "Silent Night" in 1816, but he didn't do anything with his moving poem until two years later on Christmas Eve, 1818. He turned to his organist Franz Gruber and asked him to set it to music for two voices and a guitar. Mohr sang the tenor lead, and Gruber sang bass and played the guitar. According to some sources, a choir of girls from the village joined in the melody.

Why Mohr asked Gruber to write the music may be fiction. According to several sources, on Christmas Eve, with a traditional midnight mass pending, Mohr discovered that the organ had broken down. Distraught, he went to Gruber and told him about the musical disaster. Mohr asked if he could write something without organ accompaniment, and Gruber agreed. Gruber took Mohr's words and supplied the tune; thus, we have "Silent Night."

If that part of the narrative may be legend, the rest of the story is factual. "Silent Night, Holy Night" did not win immediate and widespread acclaim. Gruber was a good old sort and gave his carol to anyone who was interested—often without even putting his name on it. The artisan who came to repair the organ, Karl Mauracher, received a copy and began spreading it to other towns. Then the Strasser Singers got a hold of it; they were a nineteenth-century version of the Trapp Family Singers of *The Sound of Music* fame. The Strasser Singers called it "The Song from Heaven" and sang it at the Leipzig Fair in 1831. In 1838, it was published for the first time in a German hymnal and described as a "hymn of unknown origin."

In 1854 the King of Prussia, Frederick William IV, heard it when it was sung by the entire choir of the Imperial Church in Berlin. He stipulated that henceforth "Silent Night" should be the first piece in all the Christmas concerts of the land. Finally, the humble Gruber wrote a letter to Berlin, clarifying that he indeed was the composer and Mohr was the author.

Even an imperial endorsement didn't make the carol popular beyond Germany. It appeared for the first time in English in 1859, but it graced few English-language hymnbooks until the twentieth century.

Because its home and initial fame was in Germany, "Silent Night" ("Stille Nacht, Heilige Nacht") played an important role in one of the most remarkable events in the history of warfare—the Christmas Truce of 1914.

World War I broke out in August 1914. One month later in the First Battle of the Marne, which lasted merely one week, there were 263,000 casualties and 81,700 killed—British, French, and German. Trench warfare soon became a military strategy for both Germany and the Allies. It was a horrific experience to be stationed in the trenches. One German soldier described the ditches as "lice, rats, barbed wire, fleas, shells, bombs, underground caves, corpses, blood, liquor, mice, cats, artillery, filth, bullets, mortars, fire, steel: that's what war is. It is the work of the devil."

By Christmas 1914 World War I had been waged for only five months. Even at that early stage, soldiers on both sides wondered why they were fighting—a doubt that lingered throughout the long conflict and ever after. On Christmas Eve, at various locations on the Western front, the British and French troops saw a spectacular sight. Here is how a German soldier reported it: "We marched forward to the trenches like Father Christmas with parcels hanging from us. All was quiet. No shooting. Little snow. We placed a tiny Christmas tree in our dugout—the company commander, myself, the [other] lieutenant, and the two orderlies. We placed a second lighted tree on the parapet. Then we began to sing our old Christmas songs: 'Stille Nacht, Heilige Nacht' and 'O du fröliche' ['Oh, How Joyfully']."

The British were stunned. One English soldier recalled later, "It was a beautiful moonlit night, frost on the ground, white almost everywhere; and . . . there was a lot of commotion in the German trenches and then there were those lights—I don't know what they were. And then they sang 'Silent Night,'—'Stille Nacht.' I shall never forget it. It was one of the highlights of my life."

During the Christmas Eve truce soldiers fraternized, sang to each other, exchanged gifts of tobacco and alcohol and chocolate and treasures from home. They played soccer with beef ration tins and even gave each other buttons from their uniforms. They also buried the dead—those who could not be reached between the trenches.

It is unclear how extensive the Christmas Truce of 1914 actually was, but most historians agree it was fairly widespread and extended even to the Eastern front. Informal truces during World War I followed, much to the dismay of the commanding officers (Stanley Weintraub, *The Story of the World War I Christmas Truce*). The cessation of fighting had little lasting political or military effect, but as one historian has written, "The December 1914 Christmas Truces can be seen as not unique, but as the most dramatic example of non-cooperation with the war spirit that included refusal to fight, unofficial truces, mutinies, strikes, and peace protests."

The story of the *composition* of "Silent Night" embodies a simple but profound truth about Christmas: out of something broken God can inspire something perfect. The story of the *singing* of "Silent Night" on Christmas Eve 1914 captures the aspiration of the human heart and the divine design for human life: "God will dwell with them, and they shall be his people, and God himself will be with them; he will wipe away every tear from their eyes, and death shall be no more, neither shall there be mourning nor crying nor pain any more, for the former things have passed away" (Rev 21:3–4).

MEDITATION

The Christmas Truce

My coauthor has written about the surprising truce that took place between German and British soldiers on Christmas of 1914. Upon closer historical inquiry, it turns out that there were other smaller manifestations of such truce-making besides that which took place on that one day. Despite the determination of generals and commanders who ordered that hostilities continue without interruption, soldiers in the trenches simply did not want to be in such a state of continuous warfare. The various truces seem to indicate that warfare is not so much the natural state of human nature as is often supposed. My concern, however, is to reflect upon the Christmas Truce within another context.

It is a common experience of pastors that the months of January and February see a rise in the number of parishioners who seek pastoral counseling. It is as though the holiday truce is over and they have now returned to their trenches to face some hostile personal situations that were temporarily suspended for the festive season of the year. Beginning with Thanksgiving Day and continuing through Christmas, the problems they faced at home or work were, for a season, "put on hold."

Come January, however, the marriage conflict has returned, the teenager with a problem is still difficult, the atmosphere at the workplace has worsened, or their personal depression has deepened. Some of the situations brought before a pastor in the drab, dark days of winter are genuinely serious and require continuing professional therapy. Many others, however, do not, so that this annual return to pastoral care raises the question of why it is that, year after year, the magic of the Christmas Truce cannot be sustained when the spiritual slush and snow of midwinter sets in.

It may be time to consider the real location of the warfare to which some of us habitually return. The battle, after all, may not be with those difficult people whom we label as the enemy. It is entirely possible that the enemy may be within. Blaise Pascal, the seventeenth-century Christian philosopher, offered a probing word upon the conflict within us. "For man holds an inward talk with his self alone, which it behooves him to regulate well," he wrote. Did you ever reflect upon the many voices going on within yourself?

There are those speeches that we continually rehearse in preparation for some argument that we intend to win. Then there's the harsh, judgmental gossip that we are absolutely sure is going on behind our back, or so we assume. More optimistically, some of us even hear the voices of praise being offered as eulogies at our funeral, the glowing testimonials of how wonderful we were in our lifetime. Of course, we ought to be able to laugh at such ridiculous inner conversations; as an old acquaintance once said, "We would worry less about what others think of us if we realized how seldom they do." Many of us, however, are unable to dispense with our negative inner chatter so easily.

So we may need serious spiritual help in regulating the many voices of our many selves. Pascal continues, "We must keep silence as much as possible and talk with ourselves only of God, whom we know to be true; and thus we convince ourselves of the truth."

I do not know why it is that silence is healing. The healing power of silence is so effective that one of the Desert Fathers, Abbot Pastor, said, "Any trial whatever that comes to you can be conquered by silence." What seems to happen in silence is that I begin to realize what can and cannot be changed. Specifically, I realize that I cannot change others, but that I can, by God's grace, begin to change myself. Free from that impossible job of fixing others, I can let God take it from there. What if silence became a regular discipline in our daily lives? I think it might work this way:

Remembering the words of the Psalmist (Ps 131:1), that I must not occupy myself with things too great and marvelous for me, I might try to remember every day, that I must not occupy myself with:

- That for which I desire to be seen, praised, recognized, or remembered as being better, holier, humbler, wealthier, or more prayerful, generous, important, interesting, intelligent, or knowledgeable than others;

- That which is pretentious, and would make me appear to be someone other than who I am by virtue of my birth and background, or my education and life experience;

- That which is not my business: the lives, choices, habits, thoughts, motives, opinions, and beliefs of others;

- That which others may think about me, remembering how seldom they do.

One of my most important spiritual mentors, C. S. Lewis, stated it this way: "The real problem of the Christian life comes where people don't usually look for it. It comes the very moment you wake up each morning. All your wishes and hopes for the day rush at you like wild animals. And the first job each morning is just shoving them all back; just listening to that other voice, taking that other point of view, letting that other larger, stronger, quieter life come flowing in. And so on, all day. Standing back from all your natural fussings and frettings, coming in out of the wind."

Down within each of us is such a "larger, stronger, quieter life." It is our normal, God-created life. We were created for such a peaceful life.

Warfare is not the natural state of affairs for which we were created. The Christmas Truce is meant to hold. The magic of Christmas is meant for all times and all seasons. Rather than tossing and turning through the night as those inner voices rage, we can leave the trenches and enjoy every night as a truly silent night.

Still, Still, Still

Still, Still, Still

A lmost by their nature, folk songs have obscure origins; usually the author of the words and the composer of the music are like psalmists—their words immortal but their creators unknown. Witness the folk carols in this book—"Go, Tell It on the Mountain" (pp. 38–43), "I Wonder as I Wander" (pp. 58–63), "Mary Had a Baby" (pp. 96–102), or "Rise Up, Shepherd, and Follow" (pp. 127–34). "Still, Still, Still" is another folk carol, and like the others, we don't know who the author and the composer might have been.

It sounds a bit like "Edelweiss" from *The Sound of Music*, and the connection is more than imaginary. "Still, Still, Still" comes from the region around Salzburg, Austria. It was first published in 1865 in a collection of folk songs, edited by Maria Vinzenz Süß (1802–1868), who was the distinguished founder of the Salzburg Museum. That Museum started out as a repository of military memorabilia and became a multi-faceted and award-winning conservatory of the art and history of the Salzburg region. The original German version had six verses, which follow the pattern of the two verses contained in English-language hymnbooks (there are several English translations).

The version we use here was translated by the American George K. Evans (1917–), a director of choirs in high schools, colleges, and churches. The music was arranged by Walter Ehret (1918–2009), "the man with a thousand voices." He arranged and published music with hundreds of pseudonyms during a career of more than fifty years. A graduate of the Julliard School of Music, Ehret directed music groups and composed or arranged more than 1,000 choral arrangements. Evans and Ehret collaborated on "Still, Still, Still" for publication in *The International Book of Carols* (1963), and since then it has become widely known.

Its popularity lies primarily in its performance, not in congregational singing. According to hymnary.org, it has appeared in a mere nine English-language hymnbooks. But it can be readily heard (sometimes with different words) in recordings by the Mormon Tabernacle Choir, the Vienna Boys Choir, Mannheim Steamroller, and Amy Carpenter, among others.

Perhaps that is how it should be, for "Still, Still, Still" is more than a carol. It is also a lullaby. Rather than singing it ourselves, it should be heard. Amidst the frenetic pace and the cacophony of sounds of the modern-day Christmas, it's ironic that we are celebrating the birth of the Prince of Peace. But if we stop long enough, we might recover the art of listening and hear the maternal reassurance of God.

MEDITATION

Carrying the Silence

There's a tiny postcard I use as a bookmark in a devotional book I've been using for more than twenty-five years. It's a colored photo of the original entrance to the now well-known Abbey of Gethsemane in Kentucky. Over the doorway are the words PAX INTRANTIBUS (Peace to Those Who Enter). Visitors no longer enter the abbey through that door, but it was through that former entryway that the now-famous Thomas Merton passed when he arrived to begin his new life as a Trappist monk on the night of December 10, 1941. He had come to stay, but my friend John and I had come only for a day.

We had visited Gethsemane on previous occasions, but this time would be different. We wanted to see what it would be like to live through an entire monastic day, to keep the same schedule as that which the brothers do on every day of their life. I wondered if I'd have the stamina to make it because I arrived exhausted from a speaking engagement at a somewhat stressful event elsewhere. To keep the monk's schedule, we would arise in the middle of the night for vigils, the first prayers of the day at 3:15 a.m. Could I make it through the entire day until compline, the last prayers of the day at 7:30 p.m.? Well, I did, but that's another story.

One of the most memorable events of the day was an afternoon walk in the abbey cemetery, during which, as you can guess, we stood in silence for some time at Merton's grave. His body had been flown back to the abbey following his accidental death in Bangkok on December 10, 1968, the very anniversary of his entrance into Benedictine life twenty-seven years earlier. As we stood there, John said to me, "If only we could carry this silence with us." Then, not long afterward, John sent this postcard with a tiny note on it, "Thinking of you today, Memorial Day, and, Morgan, carrying the silence." It will make all the difference in your life if you can learn to carry the silence with you.

Still, Still, Still is an Austrian carol that is seldom sung in our churches. I wanted to include it in our collection, mostly because of personal memories that it evokes. Toward the end of the Christmas Eve service in one of my happiest interim pastorates, the choir would sing its two short verses, over and over, during the lighting of candles by the congregation. It was almost what one would call "mood music." But it was always a special moment for me, and I'm sure also, for many pastors. At the end of the Christmas Eve service, a pastor has made it halfway through the church year (not the official liturgical year, but the preaching pastor's year). If you've made it through Christmas, now you're headed for Easter and springtime, and not too long after that, you'll arrive at your summer vacation. Pastors reading this meditation will know what I mean. But a pastor needs this special stillness of Christmas for reasons other than that.

Christmas Eve is not all stillness in many homes. Just when a pastor has arrived home to enjoy some well-earned Christmas quietness, there comes a call from a troubled home. "Wine makes life merry," wrote one Hebrew sage (Eccl 10:19), but too much wine turns the merriment into anger, answered another wisdom writer: "Wine is a mocker and strong drink is a brawler" (Prov 20:1). I'm certainly not the only pastor who has been called out late on the night before Christmas to try being a peacemaker in a home where strong drink has awakened old, unresolved hatreds.

Then too, the angel of death doesn't arrive with regard to our liturgical calendars. People die on Christmas Eve or Christmas Day. I remember being called at dawn on Christmas morning to hasten to a home where the father had died during the night, leaving a young mother to face the future alone with two small children. What was that Christmas (and many thereafter) like for those little kids? Not much of a Christmas present for them, to say the least! So a pastor's heart needs the stillness of Christmas throughout the year. Whenever we sing *Still, Still, Still*, I sense the snows of winter falling gently, and I often need those snows in the midst of summer. A tiny framed favorite winter painting by Maxfield Parrish sits next to my computer. I need the reminder of its snowy silence at many "hot" moments throughout the year—and so do you!

I'm sure that, as you've been reading these words, some words of Scripture have come back to you, such as, "Be still, and know that I am God" (Ps 46:10), or best of all, "Peace! Be still!" (Mark 4:39), Jesus' words to the winds and waves, and also to us. We'll especially need to hear those words when some storm is raging around us and God seems asleep, just as Jesus was asleep that night in the back of the boat. Here's one from the famous missionary to India, Amy Carmichael (1867–1951), that I carry with me for those time when it's hard to carry the silence with me:

> Thou art the Lord who slept upon the pillow,
> Thou art the Lord who soothed the furious sea,
> What matter beating wind and tossing billow
> If only we are in the boat with Thee?
> Hold us in quiet through the age-long minute
> While Thou art silent, and the wind is shrill:
> Can the boat sink while Thou, dear Lord, art in it?
> Can the heart faint that waiteth on Thy Will?

Use whatever imagery will help you carry the silence. Picture yourself in the boat that night with Jesus and those disciples, then repeat his words, "Peace be still," to yourself. Or try remembering that in the high mountains of the world of the Spirit, it's always snowing, even in summer, so you can always be singing that Austrian carol's three words, "Still, still, still." I even wonder if we'll have some snowy days up in heaven. I wouldn't want to live where it never snows.

The First Nowell

1 The first Now-ell the an-gel did say was to cer-tain poor
2 They look-ed up and saw a star shin-ing in the
3 And by the light of that same star three wise men
4 This star drew nigh to the north-west; o'er Beth - le -

shep-herds in fields as they lay, in fields where they lay keep-ing
east be-yond them far; and to the earth it gave
came from coun - try far; to seek for a king was their
hem it took its rest, and there it did both stop

their sheep, on a cold win-ter's night that was so deep.
great light, and so it con - tin-ued both day and night.
in - tent, and to fol - low the star wher-ev - er it went.
and stay, right o - ver the place where Je - sus lay.

Refrain

Now - ell, Now - ell, Now - ell, Now - ell,

born is the King of Is - ra - el.

5 Then entered in those wise men three,
    full reverently upon their knee,
    and offered there in his presence
    their gold, and myrrh, and
      frankincense.
    Refrain

6 Then let us all with one accord
    sing praises to our heavenly Lord,
    that hath made heaven and earth of nought,
    and with his blood our life hath bought.
    Refrain

The First Nowell

This carol is thoroughly English, probably arising from the rural area of remote Cornwall in England during the sixteenth century. "The First Nowell" shares a place with two other famous English folk songs of the same period, "God Rest Ye Merry, Gentlemen" and "We Wish You a Merry Christmas," but it has won an enduring, international reputation as perhaps the best-known carol to come out of England.

The title has often been confusing. Sometimes listed as "The First Noel" or "The First Noël," the carol might be considered as French in origin, which is not the case. The word *nowell* was used by the famous fourteenth-century English poet Geoffrey Chaucer in his magnificent epic, *The Canterbury Tales*, and it was a joyous shout on Christmas Day. "Nowell" probably comes from an old French word, "*noël*," meaning Christmas, which comes from the Latin word "natus" or "birth." Or it might come from the French word "novella" which comes from the Latin "nova," which means "news."

Jesus said, "I am the vine, you are the branches" (John 15:5). So it is with linguistic vines and branches as well.

If "The First Nowell"—in verse and in tune—arose from English folk culture of the sixteenth century, that would truly make "The First Nowell" the oldest English carol. However, the words weren't published until 1823 by William Sandys in *Carols Ancient and Modern*, and the words and music appeared together ten years later in *Gilbert and Sandy's Carols*. Variations and improvements were made, and John Stainer (1840–1901) composed and published in 1871 the four-part hymn arrangement that we sing today. Stainer is famous for his oratorio, "The Crucifixion," with the chorus "God So Loved the World," which has been widely used in worship ever since. Less well known is that Stainer probably united the tune "Greensleeves" with the words to "What Child Is This" (pp. 162–67), making him the genius behind two Christmas classics.

No Christmas carol is inerrant. As Morgan Roberts points out below, "The First Nowell" is not scripturally accurate since the shepherds never saw a star. The original version of the carol stipulated that three shepherds came to worship Jesus, and that phrase was modified for the sake of accuracy to "certain poor shepherds." The idea of three shepherds was taken from the medieval mystery plays, where their names were Harvey, Trowle, and Tudd. Ian Bradley wryly notes that "clearly they were good Anglo-Saxons rather than Palestinians."

Furthermore, geographical geeks have pointed out that "a star shining in the east" is impossible since it would mean the three individuals (shepherds or wise men but not kings) approached Bethlehem from the Mediterranean. Hence, the New Revised Standard Version translates the wise men declaring that they have "observed his star at its rising," though it offers "in the East" as an alternative translation and as a bow to tradition.

Even the music has come in for its share of criticism. As an English folk song, "The First Nowell" has a unique tune. It is the same musical phrase repeated twice, followed by a refrain that is a variation of that phrase. In other words, the carol is basically the same music repeated three times. This prompted the twentieth-century hymnologist Erik Routley to describe the music as "rather terrible." He noted that when all the original verses (nine in total) are sung, that means folks sing the same music twenty-seven times. Routley sarcastically concluded, "It is repetitive to the point of hideous boredom."

Routley may have a point, but it has been lost on other critics who have lauded this carol's simple and yet majestic beauty. Its popularity across national borders and among generations of Christians since the nineteenth century testifies to the fact that the musical repetition is both reassuring and inspiring. For this is, after all, a carol that recites the dramatic narrative of Christ's birth and then proclaims its stunning significance for the entire world:

> Then let us all with one accord
> sing praises to our heavenly Lord,
> who hath made heaven and earth of naught,
> and with his blood our life hath bought.
> Nowell, nowell, nowell, nowell,
> Born is the King of Israel.

MEDITATION

Smelling Like the Sheep

Pope Francis has called on the world's priests to bring the healing power of God's grace to everyone in need, to stay close to the marginalized, and to be "shepherds living with the smell of the sheep." I'm guessing that the pope, having identified himself with the poor of Latin America, may have some idea of how smelly sheep actually are.

During my years at my Michigan church, I had to be a shepherd of the sheep every December. To provide sheep and lambs for our church's free one-week journey through the many meanings of Christmas, I would borrow sheep and lambs from a farm near our congregation's rural conference center, load them into a horse trailer, and bring them to the church courtyard where an average of 12,000 visitors, many of whom had never seen or touched a live lamb or sheep, would enjoy them through that week. To keep them warm through the night, I'd put them back in the trailer, park them in my driveway overnight, and return them to the church in the morning. By the end of the week, my clothing would reek with the smell of the sheep.

Whenever we sing this carol, I wonder if we ever realize how amazing it is that the first announcement of Jesus' birth was made to a group of smelly shepherds. Being a shepherd was not much of a job. A shepherd was someone who couldn't find a real job, and so he lived, ate, and slept with the herd. We may have romantic images of shepherds, but we need to deromanticize them, just as Western author, Wallace Stegner, did with our Hollywood notion of the supposedly free cowboy of Western movies and novels. He wrote, "The only freedom of a cowpoke was the freedom to quit one lousy job to accept another equally lousy job."

There were no fancy printed announcements of this birth in Bethlehem; this one came to poor workmen who couldn't even read. It came from the shining "angel of the Lord" who told them that a Savior had been born—and they *didn't*, as the hymn writer says, see a star. Instead, after the angel's message, they heard an angelic choir singing. A Savior had arrived! No wonder they went running; it was about time for God to do something to save them from the crushing taxation and poverty being inflicted upon them by the Roman Empire. Maybe under a restored economy, they would have better jobs than being captives to a herd of sheep. The salvation for which they longed was probably about better jobs.

But when they arrived, breathless, at their destination, there was no Savior—at least, not the kind they expected. All they found was a baby. Could a baby be the kind of Savior they were seeking? Could an infant in a manger start the kind of revolution that would defeat the Romans and send them "packing" back to Rome in defeat? Who's afraid of a baby? Or were they looking for the wrong kind of Savior, the wrong kind of victory?

No one needs ever be afraid of a baby—that's why God arrived in such a harmless, helpless form. The entire message of the gospel is in that babe of Bethlehem. Here's the real victory over all the hatred and bloodshed of worldly empires. The world's violence, whether national or personal, is always rooted in fear. The triumph of Christmas is plainly and simply that all our reasons for fear have been banished by a God whom no one will ever again need to fear. We'll never need to fear a God who takes the risk of entering our world as an unarmed infant. Such a God will never hurt you; such a God will never run away from you or forsake you. Such a God will be with you—no matter what!

It's easy to see why this baby came to be called the Lamb of God. Lambs don't shout, scold, or shame you. Lambs won't hurt you. Quite the opposite, lambs are vulnerable; lambs get killed, which is what happened to this Lamb. But this Lamb was the one whom God raised from the dead. You can't kill the kind of defenseless love that was incarnate in this Lamb. Kill it, crucify such love, and it rises again on the third day. Little wonder that the words "fear not" are the most repeated words in the Bible. We have nothing to fear from this babe, this Lamb.

Do people hear this simple message that came to the shepherds in our churches? Stinking shepherds probably wouldn't be welcome in our tidy sanctuaries. Our pastors and priests, vested in their liturgical bling, look more like "company men" engaged in managerial tasks (sin management for others) than like real shepherds. And their message is hardly ever the simple invitation, "Behold, the Lamb of God." It often requires an experience of painful failure to transform these princes of the pulpit into real shepherds. Like Moses, a fallen prince who was reduced to the job of shepherding his father-in-law's flocks, we won't see that same shining "angel of the Lord" in burning bushes until we really hit bottom. But then we'll be ready to proclaim a message that a lowly shepherd could understand, a plain word about the Lamb who takes away the sin of the world simply by that risky love that would die rather than not love an enemy—but then keeps rising again from the dead to love even that very enemy.

We are those who have been chosen to be shepherd-messengers who go "with haste" to tell the world of such truly good news. I can't speak with the authority of Pope Francis, but I suspect that he's on to something when he suggests that world won't begin believing us until our lives are fragrant with the smell of the sheep.

We Three Kings

1 We three kings of O - ri - ent are, bear-ing gifts we trav-erse a - far,
2 Born a king on Beth-le-hem's plain, gold I bring to crown him a - gain,
3 Frank-in-cense to of - fer have I, in - cense owns a de - i - ty nigh;
4 Myrrh is mine; its bit - ter per-fume breathes a life of gath-er-ing gloom:
5 Glo-rious now be - hold him a - rise, King and God and Sac - ri - fice;

field and foun-tain, moor and moun-tain, fol - low - ing yon - der star.
King for - ev - er, ceas-ing nev - er o - ver us all to reign.
prayer and prais-ing, voic - es rais - ing, wor - ship - ing God on high.
sor-rowing, sigh-ing, bleed-ing, dy - ing, sealed in the stone-cold tomb.
Al - le - lu - ia! Al - le - lu - ia! sounds through the earth and skies.

Refrain

O star of won-der, star of night, star with roy - al beau-ty bright,

west-ward lead-ing, still pro - ceed-ing, guide us to thy per - fect light.

We Three Kings

A t this point in our book, it should be obvious that Christmas carols are not reliable accounts of history. They are works of creativity, imagination, and often genius—inspired by texts from Scripture, church teaching, and human experience. Frequently their authors and composers disappear into the fog of history. Each carol is less a carrier of history and more an embodiment of historic truths.

"We Three Kings" beautifully illustrates the unreliability of carols as accounts of history but their trustworthiness as bearers of truth.

The carol is based on Matthew 2:1–12. Matthew spends seven verses (1:18–25) on the birth of Jesus (although admittedly he didn't write in verses; the numbers were added later), and nearly all of that is devoted to an account of Mary and Joseph. Matthew concludes cryptically, Joseph "knew her [Mary] not until she had borne a son; and he called his name Jesus." Since Matthew spent the entire first chapter on what used to be called "the begats" and the house and lineage of David, one would think he would have paid a bit more attention to the birth of the Savior of the world. But one sentence covered it. On to the wise men.

As Morgan Roberts points out below, if you follow the text from Matthew closely, there's no indication that the visitors to Jesus were kings; they were wise men. There isn't even an indication that there were three of them, though they did bring three gifts of gold, frankincense, and myrrh. Then there's "the star in the East," which has fascinated historians and astronomers for centuries and may even have some basis in fact (see Ian Bradley, *The Penguin Book of Carols*).

How then did we get to "We three kings of Orient are"? The answer lies in the marvelous and mysterious mythologies that grew up around this biblical account. The three wise men became the three kings in the Armenian Infancy Gospel of the sixth century. They were given names: Melkon (later called Melchior in Europe), the king of the Persians; Gaspar, the king of the Hindus; and Balthasar, the king of the Arabs (later he was portrayed as a black-skinned man from Ethiopia, especially in Renaissance paintings of the Adoration of the Magi).

The Armenian Infancy Gospel expanded and elaborated the story considerably. The three kings on camels, it recounted, arrived from Persia with 12,000 soldiers on horseback, and they bore more than a mere three gifts. Melkon not only brought gold but also aloes, rare fabrics, and sacred books predicting the birth of Jesus and sealed by the finger of God. In addition to frankincense, Gaspar provided nard and cinnamon. Balthasar offered myrrh, plus silver, sapphires, and pearls. It was a king's bounty for the King of the Jews.

As the story of the three kings moved from the Near East into Europe, some of the trappings fell aside, and their gifts assumed symbolic power. Gaspar's gold represented the royal character of Jesus. Melchior's frankincense symbolized the worship of God in the temple and thus the divinity of Christ. Since myrrh was often used in embalming, Balthasar's present demonstrated the suffering of Christ for the salvation of the world.

Throughout the Middle Ages, the fascination with "the three kings" multiplied. When three embalmed bodies were found in the twelfth century near a church in Milan, they were declared to be the three kings, were moved to the Cologne Cathedral, and became objects of veneration and the goal of pilgrimages. One story said that the three kings designated Prester John, the central character of medieval romance, as their successor. According to other accounts, the three kings brought jewels belonging to Alexander the Great that the Queen of Sheba had taken from King Solomon's palace.

Skip forward to Advent, 1857, in New York City. There John Henry Hopkins Jr. (1820–1891), an Episcopal priest, was editing *The Church Journal*. He followed in the line of his father who was an Episcopal bishop in Vermont. Hopkins was a man of many parts and skills. During his lifetime, he was a reporter, law student, teacher, editor, priest, designer of stained glass windows, book illustrator, and perhaps most importantly for history, the first instructor in music at General Theological Seminary in New York City.

Each Christmas the Hopkins clan gathered at the family home in Vermont. John Henry Hopkins Jr. was a bachelor and adored his nieces and nephews, so as his gift for the Yuletide celebration, he sat down and wrote the words and the music to "We Three Kings." It is fairly rare to have a carol's poetry and tune written by the same person, but here it was—five verses, the first and the last to be sung by the three kings together (or a choir or a congregation) and verses two through four sung as solos by Melchior (gold), Gaspar (frankincense), and Balthasar (myrrh). Uncle Henry's composition entranced his nephews and nieces, and after its publication in 1863, it exploded in popularity on both sides of the Atlantic. As early as the 1920s, the editors of *The Oxford Book of Carols* described it as a highly successful modern example of a carol, and for millions today it is the most widely sung Christmas carol of American origin.

It is perfect for Christmas pageants with costumes and children. The baby Jesus is lying in the manger, and suddenly three regal figures come forward, steadily and slowly, to the rolling cadences of this carol's quiet, assuring melody. It sounds like the pace of three camels. And therein lies a story about my family and the three kings.

There are seven in my birth family—five girls and two boys. I think all of us participated in the annual Christmas pageant at our church (for more about that, see pp. 179–82). The part of one of the wise men was, to my memory, always played by a man named Neely Keith. He was quite tall, which fit his role as a king. He had a slight speech impediment. He and his wife had no children.

During one performance, one of my sisters (an angel in the pageant but not in real life) tottered toward the edge of the platform as three men (with train bearers) came forward to the music of "We Three Kings." Mr. Keith was climbing the stairs to pay homage to the Christ child. He saw the little girl about to plunge to what would have been certain injury, dropped his gift, lunged, and caught her. I heard him tell this story several times over the years, and on each occasion, he would choke up and tears filled his eyes.

A man who had no children wrote "We Three Kings" for children. A man who had no children but was a king saved a little girl.

Matthew's wise men, "warned in a dream not to return to Herod," who had murder on his mind, "departed to their own country by another way." Then Jesus, Joseph, and Mary fled to Egypt. And so, the wise men saved the life of a child who was yet a king.

True power protects the innocent. That's the truth.

MEDITATION

Drawn to the Light

The author of the Gospel of Matthew was taking a big risk when he included the story of the magi in his story of Jesus' birth (Matt 2:1–12). If we read the story carefully, we notice that it does not say that there were three of them, nor does it state that they came to the manger, as is usually depicted in our nativity scenes. Instead, it has them arriving about two years later, not at the manger, but at a house in Bethlehem. So what's so risky about telling this story to Matthew's audience?

Matthew is writing to a very Jewish congregation at a time when Christianity was still, for the most part, a sect of Judaism, and when most Jewish Christians were not yet ready to welcome Gentiles into their church. Thus, Matthew tells a story indicating that God's intention from the very beginning was foreshadowed in the events that surrounded the birth of the Messiah. This was a sermon that Matthew's congregation did not want to hear!

Worse yet, his story becomes all the more distasteful when it tells of how this band of uncircumcised Gentile astrologers somehow found their way to Jesus in the wrong way, along the wrong road—by following a star. Astrology was forbidden in Hebrew faith. The Law and the Prophets condemn all such divination (see Isa 47:13, for example). This is a story in which God employs pagan astrological curiosity as a means of leading people to Christ, a tale in which God ignores God's own rules in reaching out to those for whom the church will not extend a welcome!

For that matter, this story, when understood as above, will probably offend many in the church today. There is, after all, a certain satisfaction in feeling that we are the official bearers of the light, that the dark and sinful world outside of the church is dependent upon us for hearing the message, seeing the light, and being admitted to the kingdom of heaven. Indeed, many appeals to missionary service have been made upon the basis of that flattering notion. There is a high degree of ego fulfilment in thinking that we possess some influence over the eternal destiny of others.

This story, however, reminds us that there is a long arm of grace that is already reaching out to embrace the world outside of the church's orthodoxy. God is already out there in the world ahead of us, speaking words of acceptance before we have spoken, making God's love known even in those gleams of truth and beauty that are found in those other faiths.

Haven't we experienced this irresistible power of gravitational grace ourselves? Can't we all remember times when, although we weren't seeking God—maybe even running away, trying to forget God—nonetheless, some other force was holding on, pulling at us, drawing us in another Godward direction? Is that star of Bethlehem not like those supergiant stars that appear tiny to the naked eye, but which by our modern telescopes are known to be so gargantuan in gravitational force as to consume the smaller stars that come near them? The light that entered the world at Bethlehem may seem no more than a tiny speck in the limited vision of the modern world, but it is still the light that lightens every life, the mysterious force that tugs and pulls at every heart.

God's presence is inescapable. Wherever we turn, there is some hint of God's goodness, some echo of God's voice, some strain of the music of heaven. God never gives up on us. God follows us down all the pathways that we take, and meets us at every turning.

We can respond to God's inescapable light by becoming the kinds of "little lights" that reflect the ever-seeking love of God for every soul on every road. That's what the story of the magi is about. It's about the Christ of every age and place, who has always been present in our world, drawing all persons to the light. So let's be up and on our camels in all seasons, following the star to the ends of the earth, and inviting everyone else along the way to journey with us.

What Child Is This?

1 What child is this, who, laid to rest, on Mar-y's lap is sleep-ing?
2 Why lies he in such mean es - tate where ox and ass are feed-ing?
3 So bring him in-cense, gold, and myrrh; come, one and all, to own him.

Whom an-gels greet with an-thems sweet while shep-herds watch are keep-ing?
Good Chris-tian, fear; for sin-ners here the si - lent Word is plead-ing.
The King of kings sal-va-tion brings; let lov - ing hearts en-throne him.

This, this is Christ the King, whom shep-herds guard and an-gels sing;
Nails, spear, shall pierce him through; the cross be borne for me, for you.
Raise, raise the song on high. The vir - gin sings her lul - la - by.

haste, haste to bring him laud, the babe, the son of Mar - y!
Hail, hail, the Word made flesh, the babe, the son of Mar - y!
Joy, joy, for Christ is born, the babe, the son of Mar - y!

What Child Is This?

William Chatterton Dix was only in his twenties when he almost died. His illness came on suddenly and persisted, leaving him bedridden and plunging him into deep depression. Dix (1837–1898) was the manager of a maritime insurance company in Glasgow, and this dramatic reversal in his health left him helpless and adrift. He began to read the Bible avidly. His health only gradually returned, but from this near-death crisis he experienced a profound renewal of his faith.

In 1865, during his health crisis, Dix read Matthew 2:1–12, the journey of the wise men. Inspired by the account of these magi in search of Jesus, Dix wrote a poem, "The Manger Throne." Parts of it became "What Child Is This?," published in *Christmas Carols Old and New* (1871), a famous and highly influential collection edited by Henry Ramsden Bramley and John Stainer. From the same text from Matthew and out of his illness came Dix's other great composition, "As With Gladness Men of Old," usually sung during Epiphany.

At the time of his debilitating sickness, Dix was already recognized as a poet and composer of hymns. After his recovery, he continued his successful work in the insurance business, but his avocation of writing poetry became his passion and his enduring legacy. Lay people are a minority among hymn writers, but Dix wrote several volumes of poems and devotional works, a book of religious instruction for children, and hymns based on ancient Greek and Abyssinian Christian texts.

"What Child Is This?" is a poignant but eloquent poem of God's presence in the midst of suffering, but it is entirely possible that it would have had only passing popularity if it were not for its tune, "Greensleeves." Dix's editor, John Stainer, is widely credited as the one who made the almost divine combination of words and music when it was originally published. Today, according to one historian, "Greensleeves" has become "one of the most beloved pieces of music in Western civilization."

This haunting melody appeared in print anonymously twice on the same day in 1580. It was attached to secular ballads, but twelve days later it was released again as "*Greensleeves* moralized to Scripture, declaring the manifold benefits and blessings of God bestowed on sinful man." It was so well-known in the late sixteenth century that when Shakespeare wrote "The Merry Wives of Windsor," Mistress Ford refers twice to "Greensleeves," and Falstaff declares, "Let the sky rain potatoes! Let it thunder to the tune of 'Greensleeves'!"

The popularity of this folk ballad endured, but not always in religious use. During the seventeenth century, the allies of Charles I in the English Civil War used it as a party song. It appeared in John Gay's *The Beggar's Opera* (1728). In the United Kingdom, Australia, and New Zealand, the tune is frequently used as a chime on ice cream trucks. When the TV show "Lassie" was produced, the tune was played often, especially during the credits. It is also the theme of "Fantasia on 'Greensleeves,'" sometimes attributed to Ralph Vaughn Williams.

But even before Dix wrote "What Child Is This?" and ever afterwards, "Greensleeves" has been a tune for Christmas. It's a lullaby with a lilting melody and gentle rhythm that evoke the spiritual comfort and assurance Dix was seeking in his physical travail. And yet, Dix's question and focus on the poverty and pain of Christ's birth plumb the age-old question of why God became human and why Christ died. The music is comforting, but the words are probing. Dix's poetry reveals the human search for meaning which only Christ's death and resurrection will finally address:

> Why lies he in such mean estate where ox and ass are feeding?
> Good Christian, fear: for sinners here the silent Word is pleading.
> Nails, spear shall pierce him through, the cross be borne for me, for you;
> Hail, hail the Word made flesh, the babe, the son of Mary.

The events of Jesus' life are of one piece. You can't understand Christmas without Calvary and Easter, and you can't understand Christ's death and resurrection without Christmas—the Word made flesh.

There is no Christmas without Easter. There is no Easter without Christmas.

MEDITATION

Who Are You, Lord?

Here is a carol that confronts us with a question that can make all the difference in our spiritual journey, reminding us that we're all meant to be contemplatives, people who are continually looking for the deeper meaning of life. Some people think that only a special kind of personality qualifies us to become contemplatives, those odd persons who become monks and spend their lives in monasteries. But all sorts of ordinary people can be their own kind of monk or mystic. In fact, the commoner, the better. What do I mean?

We must always be asking, "What child is this?" Some people never ask this question; others spend their lives thinking about it. On my shelves are many books containing many thousands of pages devoted to one question: Who is Jesus?

For several years of my life I attended the annual meeting of the Society of Biblical Literature. It was a gathering of almost 6,000 biblical scholars whose lives are devoted to some department of biblical studies. Many of the New Testament papers presented in the 500-plus seminars explore some tiny facet of the question of who Jesus was. For the average layperson, it is mind-boggling to read the titles of how much can be written about some miniscule matter concerning Jesus.

Lest this seem a waste of time, let's remember that toward the conclusion of the Gospel of John, the author's forecast was that such a proliferation of Jesus studies would surely take place: "But there are also many other things that Jesus did; if every one of them were written down, I suppose that the world itself could not contain the books that would be written" (John 21:25).

This does not mean that the average Christian who can't read the New Testament in the original Greek is left out of the search to learn more about Jesus. Indeed, we can all be part of the quest for the real Jesus—although we should begin by realizing that there may be many more than just one "real Jesus."

So my very first suggestion is that we never settle for just one and the same Jesus. Indeed, much unhappiness has been caused by people who believe in only one Jesus. Not too long ago I attended a memorial service for a woman who had died, survived by her two children. All through her life she had told her daughter how sad it was that she (the daughter) would not be in heaven with her parents, because she didn't believe in Jesus, as they did. What the mother meant by that sad warning was that the daughter had not embraced the particular Jesus of her parents' church, a version of Jesus that was even more restricted than the Jesus of the New Testament. What was so sad was that the supposedly "lost" daughter actually believed in a much bigger Jesus, a Jesus like the one in which Trappist Thomas Merton believed, a Jesus big enough to embrace God's children of other faith traditions.

So you and I need to move around a bit and discover the Jesus who lives in the hearts and minds of God's many children. There are, I believe, as many versions of the real Jesus as there are people in the world. I don't always agree with what some people tell me about "their" Jesus, but then there are times when some humble, uneducated person tells me something about their experience of Jesus that not even the scholars have taught me. So, don't settle for just one Jesus; there's too much of him to be confined to just one person's experience.

When the Apostle Paul was confronted by Jesus in his famous experience on the road to Damascus, he asked an interesting question, "Who are you, Lord?" (Acts 9:5). If you keep reading, you discover that Paul never stopped asking that question. There is an ever-expanding understanding of Jesus that develops over the course of Paul's letters. The Paul who speaks of Jesus to the Thessalonians in the heavy, cataclysmic language of Jewish apocalyptic is not the same Paul who speaks with more sophisticated, poetic wisdom to the Athenians on Mars Hill. And that Paul is not the one who comes to the final simplicity of telling the Corinthians, "I decided to know nothing among you except Jesus Christ, and him crucified" (1 Cor 2:2).

Having a vital relationship with Jesus is like having a vibrant, growing relationship with another human being. On every morning of my married life, I need to begin my day by asking, "Who are you, Nora?" There's always more to Nora, and more to every other child of God, that can be known and loved if we keep ourselves open to the richness, wonder, and variety of human personality. For that matter, when we lose that sense of wonder about one another, our relationships begin to deteriorate.

As a pastor, I've watched all too many marriages fall apart simple because one or both partners had decided that there was nothing more to be known and enjoyed about the other. "That's the way she is and she'll never change," says the husband who has given up on the marriage. "He said it, and that's what I've come to expect from him," says the despairing wife. No relationship, especially our relationship with Jesus, will have depth, meaning, and freshness if we stop asking, "Who are you?"

So keep moving on in your relationship with Jesus. Look for him in different people and in different places. He's not a prisoner of any church; he's walking all over the world, and you may even find him in what some call the wrong places. "To reach something good, it is useful to have gone astray," wrote Theresa of Avila. Keep on questing on every day in every place and in every life. Jesus is alive and with us still today.

Don't forget that you may very likely find him in the faces of the little kids in your neighborhood, so when you meet them, be sure to say in your heart of hearts, "What child is this?" It just may be that a new little Jesus has been born, right there in your same old neighborhood.

While Shepherds Watched Their Flock

1 While shep-herds watched their flocks by night, all seat-ed
2 "Fear not!" said he, for might-y dread had seized their
3 "To you, in Da-vid's town, this day is born of
4 "The heaven-ly babe you there shall find to hu-man
5 Thus spoke the ser - aph, and forth-with ap - peared a
6 "All glo-ry be to God on high, and to the

on the ground, the an - gel of the Lord came down,
trou-bled mind; "Glad tid - ings of great joy I bring
Da - vid's line the Sav - ior, who is Christ the Lord,
view dis - played, all mean-ly wrapped in swath-ing bands,
shin - ing throng of an - gels prais-ing God, who thus
earth be peace; good will hence-forth from heaven to all

and glo - ry shone a - round, and glo - ry shone a - round.
to you and hu - man - kind, to you and hu - man - kind.
and this shall be the sign, and this shall be the sign:
and in a man - ger laid, and in a man - ger laid."
ad - dressed their joy - ful song, ad - dressed their joy - ful song:
be - gin and nev - er cease, be - gin and nev - er cease!"

While Shepherds Watched Their Flocks

I t may come as quite a shock, but aside from Jesus and Mary—and maybe angels—shepherds are the primary characters in our collection of Christmas carols. Here they are again in "While Shepherds Watched Their Flocks," which has been described as "one of the central Christmas hymns for English-speaking Protestantism since its first appearance in 1700."

Its importance for Christmas worship is underlined by the fact that for centuries in the Church of England it was "the only legally authorized Christmas hymn." As we noted earlier (pp. 77–78), the English Reformation brought with it an insistence that congregational singing had to be based on the Bible, specifically the Psalms. Eventually, Isaac Watts and Charles Wesley decisively broke the stranglehold of biblicism on English worship in the eighteenth century, and Protestants were free to exclaim, "Hark! The Herald Angels Sing!"

"While Shepherds Watched Their Flocks" helped open the gates to this revolution of sacred music and Christian adoration. It is a remarkably faithful paraphrase of Luke 2:8–14, which demonstrates that hymn writers, then and now, rarely stray far from biblical texts, language, or imagery.

It was composed by Nahum Tate (1652–1759), an Irishman described by one historian as "a man of intemperate and improvident life." Some describe Tate as having "only moderate abilities as a poet and as a playwright," but in his day he won wide recognition. He was poet laureate of England and royal historiographer. He wrote a version of Shakespeare's *King Lear* (with a happy ending) which surpassed in popularity the Bard's version in England for 150 years. But his love of alcohol and high living impoverished him, and he died in a debtor's refuge in London at the age of sixty-three.

"While Shepherds Watched Their Flocks" is his masterpiece. Tate and his colleague, Nicholas Brady (1659–1726), published a *New Version of the Psalms of David* in 1696. Four years later they released a supplement, and it was there that Tate's memorable Christmas carol appeared. The so-called *New Version* was highly controversial since it foreshadowed the arrival of hymn-singing. When one bishop was asked what he thought of a "drysalter" (one who sold dried and salted food or canned products), he sniffed, "Oh, Tate and Brady, of course." The *New Version* contained sixteen hymns; only Tate's magnificent elaboration of Luke's account has survived in contemporary use.

Given its rather tentative beginning, this carol has predictably had multiple tunes. *The New Oxford Book of Carols* in 1992 published a total of seven, but that does not exhaust the variations. In England, the tune is invariably "Winchester." In the United States and usually around the world, the carol is most often sung to music aptly called "Christmas." If Handel's "Messiah" is not the basis for "Joy to the World" (pp. 76–81), Handel was the inspiration for "Christmas." This tune was taken and revised from his obscure 1728 opera, *Siroë, King of Persia*, particularly an air described by a critic as "one of the most elegant, beautiful and pathetic, in all Handel's works."

Whatever the origin of words and music may be, "While Shepherds Watched Their Flocks," based on Luke's narrative, is an example of what is called "the perspicuity of Scripture"—the capacity of Scripture to be understood by all. According to theologian Alister McGrath, this is *Christianity's Dangerous Idea* (2007), the Protestant conviction that the interpretation of the Bible is each individual's right and responsibility.

This carol celebrates the conviction that the gospel of Jesus Christ is intended for all. It portrays impoverished shepherds who were led to worship the Christ child. Its publication was a landmark in giving common people the opportunity to sing God's praise. Its history and its contemporary power flow from the angels' pronouncement: "Be not afraid; for behold, I bring you good news of a great joy which will come to all people" (Luke 2:10).

MEDITATION

A Life of Fearless Faith

Let's begin this meditation by listing a few texts as follows:

"*Do not be afraid*, Zechariah, for your prayer has been heard. Your wife Elizabeth will bear you a son, and you will name him John" (Luke 1:13).

"Do not be afraid, Mary, for you have found favor with God. And now, you will conceive in your womb and bear a son, and you will name him Jesus" (Luke 1:30, 31).

"Joseph, son of David, *do not be afraid* to take Mary as your wife, for the child conceived in her is from the Holy Spirit" (Matthew 1:20).

"Do not be afraid; for see—I am bringing you good news of great joy for all the people: to you is born this day in the city of David a Savior" (Luke 2:10–11).

Did it ever occur to you that, from the earliest moment of his life, Jesus was surrounded by people of fearless faith? His relatives, Zachariah and Elizabeth, and his father and mother, Joseph and Mary, were all fearless people. We usually associate the word *fearless* with physically strong and courageous people. Luke, however, depicts them as (a) an elderly couple and (b) a poor young couple, who had been visited by God and who, because of that, lived with trust, rather than in fear of an angry God.

Let's remember that, although we believe in the divinity of Jesus, there were also human influences that were formative in the upbringing of his earliest years. Is it any wonder then that, from such a family of faith, there would come one who would summarize such a life of confident faith in what we call the Sermon on the Mount? When we consider the kind of living to which it calls us, could it not be entitled, *A Life of Fearless Faith*? Reflect upon just a few of its timeless truths from the Gospel of Matthew:

- The guiding purpose of such a faith is to live and act in the realization of the rule of God on earth. "Thy kingdom come; thy will be done on earth" (6:10) is the goal of such a life. The religion of Jesus was not one in which "getting into heaven" was the sole purpose of life. Quite the contrary, we are to live and act so as to bring heaven down to earth, to make the world what it would be like with God as its king. This, of course, is a reversal of what much of Christianity has become.

- It is, instead, a merciful life of peacemaking (5:7, 9), free of murderous anger, and one in which marriage is sacred (5:31–32). The most radical demand of this lifestyle is love of enemies, because God showers grace upon them and "makes his sun rise on the evil and on the good, and sends rain on the righteous and the unrighteous" (5:45). Realizing that God must surely obey his own commandments, this command assures us that God has no enemies. In such a friendly world, we need not store up earthly treasures (6:19) but can live free from worry (6:25–32).

- It was into a world of slavery, poverty, cruelty, injustice, and moral debauchery that the good news of such a sunny, cheerful, and fear-free faith arrived. We need not wonder why multitudes of oppressed and enslaved folk embraced it with joy and enthusiasm. For the first four centuries, the hope of such a world-family of faith under the father-hood of God breathed new life into a world weary of sin and darkness. For the proclamation of such a faith, the followers of Jesus' way of life endured savage persecution joyfully. Faced with death, they had that other promise to the first disciples, "Do not be afraid; I know that you are looking for Jesus who was crucified. He is not here; for he has been raised," (28:5, 6), and that final one, "Do not be afraid; I am the first and the last" (Rev 1:17).

But then, what looked at first to be the best thing, turned out to be the worst; Christianity received legal status under Constantine and, over time, the church became the kind of worldly religious institution against which Jesus had rebelled in his day. The church became the gatekeeper of a religious system that purported to save its members from a fearsome God about whom Jesus had never spoken. This dark age of the church was not even ended by the Protestant Reformation. Heralds of this terrifying God can still be heard today from the pulpits of some denominations.

But there were quiet rebellions that sought to bring the church back to the fear-free good news of Jesus. The one with which most of us may be acquainted was that led by Francis of Assisi. As a "dropout" from the suc-cess and economic agendas of both the church and the world, Francesco de Bernardone (1182–1226) set out to live again by the high ground values of the Sermon on the Mount. Thanks to him and his friend Chiara Offreduc-cio (St. Clare, who founded the Order of Poor Ladies), a period of new gospel life was realized again. Such grand moments never last long in their "first, fine, careless rapture," but something always remains.

Just as it was with the first followers of Jesus, the Franciscan way of life is deceivingly simple, but terrifying in its demands. If you want to be a true follower of Jesus or of someone like Francis, get ready for sacrifice, suffering, and controversy. Just living by that commandment "Love your enemies" can make *you* the enemy in any age. That's why the sad remains of that way of life has been called "birdbath Franciscanism," a beautiful counterfeit practiced by those who have expensive statues of St. Francis in highly manicured gardens, but live by worldly, violent values against which both Jesus and Francis rebelled.

So there's your challenge as you live through another Christmas season. The angel's words, "Fear not!," can still be realized in your life. The simple beauty of life on the mount with Jesus, or the rich poverty of life with Francis, can be yours today. I wish you such a deeper, truly fear-free Christmas!

O Holy Night

Introduction/Interlude

1 O ho - ly night, the stars are bright-ly shin - ing, it is the night of the dear Sav-ior's birth. Long lay the world in sin and er - ror pin - ing, till he ap-peared and the soul felt its worth. A thrill of hope the

2 Led by the light of faith se - rene - ly beam - ing, with glow-ing heart by his cra - dle we stand. So led by light of a star sweet-ly gleam - ing, here came the wise men from the O - rient land. The King of kings lay

3 Tru - ly he taught us to love one an - oth - er; his law is love and his gos - pel is peace. Chains shall he break, for the slave is our broth - er, and in his name all op - pres - sion shall cease. Sweet hymns of joy in

wea-ry world re-joic - es, for yon-der breaks a new and glo-rious morn!
thus in low-ly man-ger, in all our tri-als born to be our friend;
grate-ful cho-rus rais-ing, let all with-in us praise his ho-ly name.

Fall on your knees! O hear the an - gel voic - es! O
he knows our need, he guards us from all dan - ger. Be -
Christ is the Lord! O praise his name for - ev - er! His

night di - vine! O night when Christ was born! O
hold your King; be - fore him low-ly bend! Be -
power and glo - ry ev - er-more pro - claim! His

1, 2

night di - vine! O night, O night di - vine!
hold your King; be - fore him low-ly bend!
power and

3

glo - ry ev - er-more pro - claim!

176

CONCLUSION

O Holy Night

My colleague Morgan Roberts and I decided to make this carol the conclusion of our book, and Morgan honored me by asking me to write it, principally because it figures prominently in a story about my childhood. More about that later.

First, consider the history of this "brilliant and polished French carol," "Cantique de Noël," that "appears to be without blemish or defect," according to Christmas carol expert William E. Studwell.

The words were written by Placide Cappeau (1808–1877), a wine merchant and poet in Provençal, France. When he was eight years old, he was playing with a friend who brandished a gun and shot Cappeau in the hand. He was gravely injured and the hand was amputated; out of remorse, his friend's father underwrote part of his education. Despite his handicap, Cappeau received the first prize in drawing from the Collège Royal d'Avignon, went on to receive a degree in literature in Nimes, studied law in Paris, and was licensed as a lawyer in 1831.

He returned to the family home in Roquemaure, near Avignon, and entered his father's business of selling wines and spirits and pursued his avocation in literature. In 1847, the parish priest asked him to write a poem for Christmas. Since Cappeau was leaving for Paris on a business trip, the priest asked that he give the poem to the distinguished composer Adolphe Adam (1803–1856) for the music to accompany the words. According to Cappeau, he was inspired to write the words in his carriage on December 3, 1847 with the title, "Minuit, Chrétiens" (or "Midnight, Christians"). Although Cappeau later received literary recognition, at that point, he was an unknown poet asking a great composer for assistance. Adam had recently written the ballet *Giselle* to wide acclaim, both then and today, but he obliged Cappeau. A couple of days later, Adam delivered the gorgeous music of "Cantique de Noël," and it was performed for the first time a few weeks later in Roquemaure at the midnight Christmas Mass.

In 1855, the carol was translated into "O Holy Night" by the American John Sullivan Dwight (1813–1893). He was educated at Harvard as a Unitarian minister, lived at the transcendentalist community of Brook Farm and directed its school for six years, and then devoted himself to music and journalism. A lover of Beethoven, he became the first significant music critic in United States history.

Here the plot thickens. Despite its initial popularity in France (among the population but not the church) and its translation into many languages, "Cantique de Noël" became controversial. The author Cappeau may have been a somewhat conventional Roman Catholic when he wrote his poem; otherwise, his priest would not have asked him to write it. But he later became a political radical of his day, opposing "inequality, slavery, injustice, and all kinds of oppression" (Studwell). He eventually renounced his work entirely and indeed Christianity itself. The theology of his "Minuit, Chrétiens" is utterly orthodox, but the seeds of his later political views do emerge. For example, a literal translation of the poem into English identifies Christmas as

> . . . the solemn hour,
> When God as man descended unto us
> To erase the stain of original sin
> And to end the wrath of His Father.
> The entire world thrills with hope
> On this night that gives it a Savior.

Subsequent verses, however, draw out Coppeau's implications of the incarnation:

> . . . O mighty ones of today, proud of your greatness,
> It is to your pride that God preaches.
> Bow your heads before the Redeemer!

Or, even more pointedly, especially at a time before the American Civil War and emancipation:

> The Redeemer has broken every bond:
> The earth is free, and Heaven is open.
> He sees a brother where there was only a slave,
> Love unites those that iron had chained. . . .

> People, stand up! Sing of your deliverance,
> Christmas, Christmas, sing of the Redeemer!

Dwight's sanitized translation—indeed, his entire rewriting—of Cappeau's poem as "O Holy Night" makes it both religiously acceptable and politically neutral, but the fact is that "O Holy Night" appears in only thirty-seven English hymnbooks, according to hymnary.org.

The explanation may be that the carol is difficult for congregations to sing. It does soar and covers a wide range of the scale. I find it difficult to sing, but that is due principally to the absence of my musical skill. At least part of the story may involve historic prejudice and theological acrimony. The composer Adam was a Jew. The poet Cappeau became an atheist and political leftist. The translator Dwight was a Unitarian. This was hardly a lineage that commended the carol to Christians for widespread Christmas use.

That's not a pretty story in the twenty-first century, but the story of "O Holy Night" is elegantly ironic. For all the greatness of the ballet *Giselle*, Adam's place in history is secured by his music for "O Holy Night." Cappeau would be a footnote in French political history except for his poem. Dwight's music criticism has antiquarian interest, but his English rendering of "O Holy Night" is for the ages. Perhaps the supreme irony, not unknown in the history of church music, is that something profoundly beautiful and Christian should come from "outside the camp" (Heb 13:13).

≠

Now my story. I was baptized, confirmed, and ordained as a minister in the Fourth Presbyterian Church of Chicago. It was and is a very large church that has resisted the decline and death of downtown churches through superb preaching, exquisite music, and compassionate ministry to its city and beyond. The building is an elegant neo-Gothic edifice. Today its steeple is overshadowed by the skyscrapers around it, but in my youth it dominated the skyline of north Michigan Avenue. Fourth unabashedly calls itself "a light to the city," and it is all of that. Even though I haven't lived in Chicago for more than a half-century, Fourth was and in many ways still is "my home church."

The Mulder family consists of seven children—five girls and two boys. We lived forty-five minutes from Fourth Church in a heavily Catholic neighborhood. It was more difficult to get to Fourth Presbyterian Church than be accepted by our neighbors, because my parents acted like pre-Vatican II Catholics in having such a large brood.

As we were growing up, Fourth Church staged a Christmas pageant each year, directed by Alice Bowles, a young woman with theatrical training. It was a spectacle—stage lighting, music guided by a professional organist and choir director and singing by professional soloists, biblical-era but contemporary-sewn costumes, and makeup. Carpenters constructed a stage across the entire nave, and there were many rehearsals (a strain on my parents, who had to make the long journey midweek for their children to act out their parts). The only thing missing was live animals or even costumed humans pretending to be sheep and camels. The dramatic script was entirely biblical, narrated by people with sonorous voices, and Christmas carols enriched the narrative.

All seven of us Mulder children had roles in the Christmas pageant. We graduated from one part to another. I started as a little angel when I was small, then moved to being a shepherd boy and a train bearer for the wise men, and finally to a full-fledged angel. As far as I can remember, none of us played the big roles—Mary, Joseph, the shepherds, the wise men, and certainly not Jesus. He was always a doll.

I remember much of the pageant, but there are two moments that I vividly recollect. One was the annunciation to Mary. A plainly dressed peasant girl, she discovers that she will bear a child. She is alone on stage—surprised and shocked. Suddenly a spotlight shines on a soprano angel in the pulpit, who sings, "Fear not, Mary, for thou hast found favor with God." That divine assurance—"fear not"—became a vital part of my faith and piety throughout my life as I have struggled with recurring insecurity and suppressed fears.

The second involved the whole cast. Baby Jesus was in the manger, lovingly watched by Mary and Joseph. The shepherds had arrived. The wise men had trooped from the back of the sanctuary (a long ways, probably 150 feet) to the stage. The angels, large and little, surrounded all the other players. Then a soloist began to sing, "O Holy Night, the stars are brightly shining." When it came to the line, "Fall on your knees!," that's what we all did. And then everyone slowly raised their arms and hands toward heaven as the soloist continued,

> O hear the angel voices!
> O night divine!

O night when Christ was born!

O night divine!

O night, O night divine!

I loved that part. It was so beautiful.

When I was about ten, I think I was a shepherd boy. At home we had a huge Magnavox console, which we all thought was magnificent. It had an AM/FM radio, a three-speed turntable (33 1/3, 45, 78), and a Formica top so our drinking glasses didn't leave a mark. We also had a respectable collection of Christmas carol records. One afternoon after school, I put on a recording of carols, including "O Holy Night." Maybe I thought I was rehearsing my part, but I think something more was at stake.

When I heard, "Fall on your knees," I did. As a choir sang, "O hear the angel voices!" I raised my arms and hands toward the ceiling. Suddenly, one of my sisters came into the living room, saw her brother on his knees with his arms extended to heaven, and laughed. Yes, she laughed. I remember how embarrassed I was, but I protested that I was simply rehearsing. It had no impact on her. Still giggling, she left me alone.

Even at the time, I didn't resent her—much. That experience of praising God on a holy night—on stage and at home—stayed with me. It was reverence that motivated me to do it, and it was awe that I experienced. Many years later, I was asked which book had most influenced my theology. I listed Rudolph Otto's *The Idea of the Holy* (1917), a classic exposition of what Otto called "the numinous"—a "non-rational, non-sensory experience or feeling whose primary and immediate object is outside the self."

We often speak of "a childlike awe" and properly so. I think it's harder for us as adults to admit to weakness and submit to "a power greater than ourselves." In fact, I think my most pronounced spiritual and behavioral failings are rooted in my inability to remember the awe I felt as a young boy hearing "O Holy Night." Children are good at awe. Like me, adults too often leave it behind.

I am convinced that the heart of Christmas is awe—the conscious and unconscious wonder at a powerful God who became a baby, a magnificent deity born in poverty, and an unconditional love that embraces us as we are, wherever we are.

When he was three years old, my grandson Sean asked me—apropos of absolutely nothing—"Grandpa, what is God?" I gulped. After all the years of teaching, preaching, and writing about God, I needed an answer—one that a three-year-old would understand. "God is love," I stammered, "great, big, stupendous love, larger than the universe."

"Oh," he said.

I think he may have understood. "Oh." That's what Christmas is all about.

T. S. Eliot wrote in "Little Gidding":

> We shall not cease from exploration.
>
> And the end of all our exploring
>
> will be to arrive where we started
>
> and know the place for the first time.

Jesus said, "Unless you turn and become like children, you will never enter the kingdom of heaven" (Matthew 18:3).

It's easy to fall on your knees when you're a child. It's harder when you're an adult, and even harder to get up. That's the point: "Fall on your knees! O hear the angel voices!"